# The Girl

## WHO CRIED DADDY

# The Girl

## WHO CRIED DADDY

*Melinda Clark*

**The Girl Who Cried Daddy**
Copyright © 2018 by Melinda Clark

Library of Congress Control Number:     2018959158
ISBN-13:    Paperback:     978-1-64398-420-9

Printed in the United States of America

LitFire LLC
1-800-511-9787
www.litfirepublishing.com
order@litfirepublishing.com

**`THE GIRL WHO CRIED DADDY'** IS THE TITLE OF THIS BOOK.
I'm dedicating it to my late father, Bishop Perry Smith. The subtitle
is the Preacher's Daughter. I was a motherless child and this book
is also dedicated to my Deceased Mother Virginia, who passed at
age 24, I never got to know my mom. My life was hard as a female
child. I was the only girl of three siblings growing up on the
westside of Atlanta. My mother died when I was 13 months old.
Franklin the eldest son, was only 3 years old when our mom
passed, my oldest brother says that he remembered our mom
somewhat, my baby brother Stevie was only 1 year old, and says
he doesn't remember her either.  But all 3 of us have had dreams of
my mother,  my dad used to tell us she was our angel, always
watching after us, because she loved her children. Once I started
staying with my father and two brothers at the age of 11, I learned

that my dad had a high temper, and used to get into fights with other people, when he was hanging out in bars, and liquor houses, as they were called back in the 70, and he didn't know how to care for his only a daughter, so I was given to another married couple, who had lost their only child to a disease called yellow fever. My dad had just become a preacher, when him and another Bishop came to get me from my step parents' house, my dad used to leave us home alone, while he go and attend to his church, he had just started his church in Atlanta, a lot of members he picked up for church, because some of them didn't have a car to drive, but before he leave home, he'd always give us money to buy krystal burgers, and told us to walk up to Krystal before it got dark, and get back in our house and lock the door, and don't open it for anyone, and he would be home later that night. We were always asleep when he returned. One Sunday night as we were on our way up the street to buy us some Krystal burgers, at that time in 1973 they were only 10 cents per burger, several big dogs started barking and chasing us! We ran until we were all most out of breath! In an instant we all heard a voice say, don't run, don't run! The Voice was so loud it scared us silly! we all looked around at each other, it was pitch black dark, some of the street lights were dim, we could barely see each other and didn't see anyone else in sight. But the dogs stopped chasing us, and they turned around as if they heard it also, we told my dad about the incident when he got back from church that night. He told us that was our mother, she was shielding us. We cried and cried because we didn't even get to know our mother. He

told us she would always be our guide through life, she's an angel with her 3 Children under her wings, me especially, because I was her only baby girl! We cried ourselves to sleep that night, we did get to know and remember her mother Loretta, our grandmother, and spent some time with her, also my grandfather William. When we were little, dad took us over to my grandparents' home for the weekend, when we arrived, Grandma Lorette would greet us with the biggest smile, and say Come on in kids, have you all eaten yet? It was her way of making us feel comfortable, telling us to make ourselves at home, as children, we loved our grandma for asking that simply question, have you eaten yet? I was glad she did ask, because I knew my brothers were not getting enough food to eat at my father's mother house where we were living, until we got our own place to live, we would always have to share everything, we had nothing of our own, so we nod our heads saying No!! We haven't eaten GrandMa Loretta, Because we knew that she would fix us something good to eat<, she asked the right question, at the right time, While staying over there we were treated like we were their kids. My grandmother was about 5;9 and weighed about 209 med skin with med length hair that she kept curled up all over, and lightly combed out, down to her shoulders, she would always get up early in the morning than anyone else in the house, and would always fix big breakfast for everybody, grits, toast, jelly, bacon and eggs, and some type of juice every morning, That might be the reason I don't eat eggs today, because I ate them so much as a child, and I only ate them when my Grandma Loretta, would fix them for

me, Grandma Loretta was a cook, and a seamstress! We would go to church on Sundays with my granddad William, grand dad was med Build, tall brown skin Man, and low cut wavy hair, he wore glasses, and always dressed nice, in casual clothes around the house, but wore a different suit to church every Sunday, my grandmother Loretta hardly ever went to the early morning service, I always remember her cooking, and sewing with her sewing Machine, that's what made me want to sew as I got Older, watching her. Before we left to go back home, on the weekends, my Granddad would always give me and my brothers an allowance of $2.00 or more. I was overwhelmed, and so happy while we were over there, I never wanted to leave, because they were so generous and kind to us, and always feed us well, no one was left hungry, or had to eat leftovers when we did leave, my dad came to pick us up on Sunday Nights, the 3 of us were full and had money in our pockets!! 3 happy little kids, and that's a lot compared to where we had came from, and where we were going back to, my brothers would get whippings for being bad and not telling the truth sometimes, although my grandparents Loretta and William never had to whip me because I never did anything bad enough to get one. One weekend we spent over there, later that evening I was watching my grandma make some curtains, so before we left that weekend, grandma called me into her sewing room, and to my surprise gave me her sewing machine! I was so amazed, I could not believe it, because I was always watching her sew. As a girl I just wanted to know how to make clothes & things, so When I got

4

bigger around 11 and 12, I started trying to sew, and knit with two straws, because I didn't know how to work the sewing machine yet, One afternoon while living with my step Parent Mrs. Jett, she saw what I was trying to do, she asked my step dad took me downtown Atlanta and bought me two knitting needles, and she enrolled me in sewing classes in the after school program when she saw that I was interested, the sewing machine that my grandmother Loretta gave me when I was about 10, I'm 49 now, and I still have that sewing machine, and I still use it to do alterations, hem pants, or make curtains . As I stated before, I was a motherless child, although I did have several step parents, some that treated me fairly, and some who treated me cruel, which was my father's mother and one of his sisters, which was my Aunt Ruby, next to the baby sister of the 16 of them, my father side had a huge family, majority are ladies, I thought because I was the only girl my dad had, was the reason they treated me like I don't belong in there family. I just didn't know why! But I was only a child still learning how to cope with all these different people, and not having my biological mother to talk or to teach me anything. So, I made some mistakes along the way of life, but I did see my mother in several dreams and vision back in 1975, when me, my dad and brothers lived on Peoples street, on the west end of Atlanta, with their 2nd step mother Doris. She was my 2nd stepmother also, because I had one stepmom previous, before I came to live with my Dad and brothers, I remember her well, Her name was Mrs. Jett she was short fat, about 300 pounds, and dark skinned, but she had the

heart of gold, and always treated me like I was her only child, I felt so much love from this couple, My step Father was Mr. Wade, loved to drink his alcohol, I remember she would always tell him, don't come home from work intoxicated today Wade, because you might have to take me to the Grocery store or downtown, she never learned to drive, so she depended him to drive us wherever we needed to go, I grew up with this family from 24 months, until I was 11 years old. I was given to her by my father sister, which is my Aunt Bertha, who was the 1st Beautician of the family, she went to beauty college, and finished at a beauty shop, she gave me to this family, because my dad at that time didn't know how to raise a daughter, and was hanging out at all times of night, he wasn't responsible enough to take care for a girl. So, he and the boys lived together until he could find another lady friend or a wife to help him care for the three of us, he just didn't want his daughter to be a part of that lifestyle. He said that boys were easier to handle although they got beat a lot from dad because of his drinking, and the stress of not having our mother who died of a heart attack at the age of 24! I was on the other side of town, having a good life growing up with my step parents, going to elementary school, this couple cared for me so well I thought that these people were my biological parents, because I was too little to ask questions, or understand that my real mother had died. So as life went on I began taking up sewing in school, not knowing that the hidden talent was already in my genes, from my Grandmother and Mom. My mother was a nurse I'm told, as I got older I began taking up

Nursing not knowing that this would someday become my passion, and my career, I finished Nursing School at Ga Medical Institute, in 1993, now I'm a state Certified Nurse, I've been in the nursing field for 19 years and I love every minute of it. As a child I began to love these people that were taking care of me, I was very conscientious and look forward to going downtown on Fridays, to get my fat writing tablets, when my step father Wade got home from his job making metal, he worked on the medalyard, that's what they called it in 1969, he loved to drink his alcohol, and I learned later from my Step Mother that the liquor house was right across the street from his job!! but he still managed to take care of me and his wife my step mom Mrs. Jett, because she never worked, all I had ever saw her do was cook, and clean the house, and argue with him everyday about his drinking, once i remember he was drinking alcohol, and eating watermelon on the front porch, my step mother Mrs. Jett used to tell him stop eating Watermelon and drinking alcohol, its gonna kill you someday! she went back into the kitchen to finish cooking dinner, that Thursday evening when I looked out the front door, he asked me did I want to come out and sit with him ? I went out and sat with him on the beige brick stairs, leading from our front door, he looked up in the sky, it began to turn dust dark, and he began to sing a song called(way in the water God's gonna trouble the water)that was my first time ever hearing him sing, and the first time I heard that song, so each time he was intoxicated, he would always sing that song, later my stepmother came to the front door and said, y'all can come on in and eat dinner, so he

picked me up and carried me in the house, and told me to go wash my hands, because i was playing out on the porch, we all sat at the table and had our dinner, the next day was Friday, after I got home from elementary school, I would always be in the window on Fridays evenings looking out the window down the street, watching & waiting to see my step dad come home, so he could take us downtown, My stepmother use to tell him all the time don't come home drunk on Friday evening Wade, because you have to drive us downtown, to get those writing tablets for her, she knew I loved to write. I was only 6-years old, The writing tablets were only 25 cents,, that was in 1968-69 when Martin Luther king and Kennedy was assassinated, I remember because my stepfather said he was on the corner of Pryor St, in Downtown Atlanta waving at his friend across the street, they were having a MLK king parade that year, on pryor street going thru Auburn Ave in Atlanta Ga, and he was in the background, my stepmother Mrs. Jett saved those pictures for years, until they got misplaced as they were moving from one house to the next,. I lived with this couple from a baby until I was 11 years old, when one Sunday morning in 1974, this big long dark blue car, which I later learned that it was a cadillac pulled up in front of our house and 2 men got of the car, they both had suits on, I was in the living room playing with my new tablet, and jax stones that my step parents had just bought me that previous weekend, when I saw the men approaching the door, I got up and ran to get my stepmother Mrs. Jett, and she let them in, they began to talk about me to her . One of the men wearing a suit

was big and fat, looked about 6 feet tall, dark skinned, the other man was light brown skin, med length hair and kinda stockie build with hazel eyes, which scared me, because I had never seen anyone with eyes that color, so I ran! into the other room, my step mother yelled, don't be scared Baby, she began to tell me the fat man was a Preacher named Bishop Croom, the other man with the hazel eyes, that I was afraid of, was my biological father Perry Smith, and the preacher began to tell my step mom, that my dad had gotten his life together, that he no longer drank, or smoke cigarettes, and don't hang out in the streets anymore, he is now a deacon in his church, and that my dad has another wife now, and they wanted to talk about taking me back with them to my father's house, he told her that I had two brothers that I never saw, and I needed to get know them, my stepmother was devastated!, that was the first time I had ever saw her crying, and that made me cry, I was also disturbed and upset because I didn't understand what was going on, and why were they making me leave her! all I know is that I was her only child, and she had raised me from a baby, I was given to her right after my, biological mother Virginia had passed of a heart a tack in her early 20s, my step mother first born child had died of yellow fever back in the late 50's, whatever that was in those days I didn't know, I learned what yellow fever was once I got older, and began working as a nurse's aide in the Hospital, she began to tell them that I was all she cared and lived for, and she didn't want me to leave Her, they told her she didn't have paperwork on me, so legally I belong to my father Perry

Smith, and that I had 2 brothers that were waiting on me, and wanted to see me . I cried for days, and weeks, because I didn't want to leave her either, this is the family that I knew and loved for years, I thought these two wonderful people, were my biological parents, so that preacher Bishop Croom and my father took me anyway, of course I was Screaming and kicking,! Because I didn't want to go, I began to live with my father and my two brothers, the first week I was away from home I was sad, and always crying, I didn't want any of them to talk to me, I just wanted to go back home to Mrs. Jett, and her husband Wade, my dad and his wife at that time was Doris, which was my brothers 2$^{nd}$ stepmother, but I still didn't want to leave the family I had grown to love, the couple that had raised me, I had missed them so much I felt sick, I wanted to go back, but every time I would ask my dad to take me back, dad never let me go back to visit them, Doris which was my dad's wife at the time, was in bishop croom church also, everybody called her dotti, because she had dark skin, kind of tall, medium build a size 12, short black hair and lots of black moles on her face, once i started staying with them, I remember hearing her and my dad argue a lot, my dad would go out of town on weekends, after he had gotten him a church in Jeffersonville Ga, The church sat just across the street from a railroad track, on Highway 80, some people called it the happy spot on Highway 80, he would leave us three Children at home with her in Atlanta, soon as the word spread about a New preacher intown, he had to open another church in Danville Ga, even though it was a small wood frame house, people

still came to hear him preach! He even had a tent before he got the house church, we use to have church revivals in the tent, people would come from all over the neighborhood to see and hear him, when we went to church with my dad my oldest brother would play the guitar and my baby brother would be on the drums, He would always appoint someone to be in charge when he was away, when we didn't travel with dad there was another couple named Penny & Robert that was in his church, her husband Robert would play the drums, I used to hear my dad call Penny high yellow, and her husband Robert blackie, dad would go back and forth from out of town attending to his churches, when he returned home my brothers and I could hear him and my stepmother Doris Augring, they would argue about another lady that was in his Jeffersonville church her name was Lila, one night after dad got back from Jeffersonville, this lady Lila came back up to Atlanta with him, she and another guy spent the night at our apartment, after they left the next weekend, when dad got back home my stepmother Doris, said she was tired of my dad provoking and beating her, they argued because she accused him of cheating and dating Lila, and my father denied that he was seeing Lila, my dad told her that she was just his pastor's Aide in the church, which is the person to give the preacher water, and a clean handkerchief when needed, and handle all the church business when he's away, when Lila had broken+ up with her child's father Mr. Ronnie Bell, my stepmom Doris said that she knew that Lila was having an affair with my father, the (Bishop)because she was the only lady in his church,

that he would let drive his Lincoln and keep it overnight, she was told by other members of his church that he treated Lila as his wife, while they were at his Jeffersonville church, and when they were out to Restaurants, so one sunday night when my dad came home from preaching at his Jeffersonville church, my step mother Doris was waiting on him, she said she was going to fight him back, she had a big 2 by fore piece of wood, she had asked my older brother to get for her, she hid it behind the bedroom door, just in case dad started provoking her, she had been suspicious of him and this other lady for months, And what people were telling her while she was in Atlanta caring for us, he and Lila was always together at his Jeffersonville church, So when he got back home late one sunday night they started arguing and fighting, me and my brothers could hear them yelling and screaming at each other, we heard banging against the walls, we were scared stiff!, so we stayed in our rooms with our door closed, One day after coming home from Blalock elementary school, once me and my brothers had gotten upstairs, Doris told us that my dad was having an affair with that lady Lila which was a shapely short woman about 5 ft, and fair skinned, and a nice cola shape as they would say a brick house shape, Doris said she was mad as hell, and she took her anger out on us, whenever she was mad with my dad, he would leave home to go to his Jeffersonville church, on saturday nights, and won't come back until Sunday night, One afternoon after school, I wanted a J J hat when they first came out, the rolling store truck came around the neighborhood every day around 4 o'clock after all the kids had

gotten home from school, I ask my step mom Doris could she please buy me one of those hats, because all the other kids in our neighborhood had a JJ hat, she replied no,! I cried because I wanted one of those hats, she punished me because I went outside to the truck, just to see the other kids JJ hats, and I asked them how much were they? I called her the wicked step mom, she made me go to my room, because I was crying, 10 min later she got the salt from downstairs, and came in my room, I was wondering what was she doing with Salt? Witchcraft? I don't know I'm just a 11 year old child, She began to pour two pillars salt down on the floor, and made me kneel down on my knees in the pillars of salt for an hour and not move, my brothers felt bad for me, it was nothing they could do but cry, and tell my dad when he got back in town, when they told my dad what she had done to me, he began to question her, then they started arguing and fighting we could hear them yelling, and things banging against the walls again, soon after that, about two weeks later, when we came home from elementary school, she told us she was tired of fighting and was leaving our dad, so that weekend she left, and we 3 kids me and my two brothers were alone again, with just my father, for about 4 months without a mother, one weekend he went to Tallahassee fishing, and we stayed at home alone, when he got back home, he told me to go fry us some fish, and I went to the kitchen to prepare the fish, and fried it just like he said, I brought it upstairs to my dad, he looked at it and just shook his head in disbelief, and told me to take it back downstairs, and he would come and finish it, remember

I'm only 11 years old and no one, has taught me how to cook,, my brothers yelled upstairs to my dad, Dad! Daddy, this fish is not done!, dad replied what ! my brother yelled, this fish don't have anything on it,! dad said ok boy ! I'll be downstairs to look at it, I didn't know to put batter on the fish, or seasoning, well dad did understand, and realize that he had a daughter that was eager to learn, and now he needed another wife to help teach me how to cook, because he didn't have the time, so later in the coming year, he married that lady Lila, that him and my step mom Doris had fought about so many nights, Lila had two sons, that made it a family of 5, which she didn't bring her two sons, into our family for the first few years, they stayed in Macon her mother Mrs. Ruth, she didn't want my dad with his temper beating on her kids, No one could blame her for that, she was just protecting her kids, but no one could protect us from dad's anger, they would always find something bad to tell my dad about my oldest brother, Franklin and dad would beat him, more than he did me and my baby brother Stevie. Before our dad got married to Ms. Lila, we had to stay with my Dad's mother, which was our grandmother, Evelyn Gates, we stayed with her until my first year of high school at Brown High, I just started 8th grade, my older brother Frank was in the 9th, my baby brother under me was in the 7th, my father's mother also had her other daughter ruby kids, to keep after school also, when my grandmother would cook, the three of us noticed that she would feed my cousin them first, and that happen all the time when she cooked, we would get the leftovers, if anything was left, sometimes

they would throw whole biscuits, in the garbage also pieces of meat, and my oldest brother Franklin would be still hungry, so he would get it out, as soon as they threw it in,  and eat it, no other adult knew about it, because we would not tell on him, because if we had told my grandmother, she would beat him and then tell my dad, and we knew dad would beat him also and probably us to,  for him getting food out the trash, we were also afraid to tell dad, that we wasn't getting feed enough food,  I felt bad for my brothers, because not only did we get the leftovers, but I wore the same dark blue dress for 4 months, although it was pretty with gold buttons down the front,  my grandmother hardly ever washed it, and she didn't allow us to use her washing machine, and she never took me shopping for new clothes, the dress was dirty and sweaty, a friend of my grandmothers, came to visit her one day, he offered to buy me clothes for school, because he said he always would see me wearing that same dress, this was my first year of high school, but I told him to ask my grandmother because I was afraid to talk to men,  he asked her, and she told him no, when my dad got back in town from his Jeffersonville church, she told him I was pregnant and was begging a man for clothes, he ask her what was she doing with my deceased mother's check, and the money that he was giving her and my Aunt, that was supposed to be for our care, and not for his sisters children's, which were my cousins, he still beat me,  because she had told him I was pregnant too I was only 14 and still a virgin, I knew nothing about sex,  at age 15 and 16 I was still afraid to talk to boys or men,  and still a virgin!, I was too scared of

my father, to do anything like that because of my previous beating, and punishments I had received from my Father, and our step mother she could not defend us, because she were afraid of him also. Well since my father mother, which was my grandmother Evelyn (Ma),we called her, didn't buy me any new clothes or my brothers, I gotta clean blouse out of the hall closet, and wore it to school one morning, it was my first year of high school, and I wanted to look nice and wear something different when I got back to my class from my lunch, and started doing my work, someone knocked on the classroom door, my teacher got up from her desk to let them in, to my surprise it was my aunt ruby,! I got happy and excited, because I thought she was bringing me something nice, she had a bag in her hand, and she asked my teacher could I come with her, the teacher replied yes! Of course, so we walked down the hall to the girls bathroom, and she told me to take off her blouse, and began to ask me why ? did I get her blouse without asking, I told her because I didn't have anything clean to wear to school, and Grandma did not wash any clothes yet, and she will not let me wash was either, my aunt was very upset, and pulled an old t-shirt out of the bag for me to put on, and said she was going to tell my dad when he came from out of town, I knew I was going to get a beating from my dad, when he got back from out of town, because anything they told him about us he would beat us, weather it was the truth or not, we had no voice in the matter!, that's just how it was, I went back into my classroom, feeling scared, and sad, because I knew when I got home I was going to get a beating from

my grandmother, and another one from my dad when he got back, well I finished my work. When I got home from school, my grandmother whipped me for wearing my aunt Ruby blouse to school, when my dad got back that weekend, yea he whipped me again also, because of what my grandmother and Aunt had told him, as I got older, I later told him how we were being mistreated, we were always scared, and hungry, and not being cared for, I know he was paying them good money just for us 3 kids to stay there, because he told us so, he said sometimes he couldn't buy himself new shoes, because most of his money was going to grandma, and my aunt for keeping us, he told us not to worry, we'll be moving out into our own house soon, the next year things gotten a little better, we did move into our own house with his new wife Lila, and her sister Carolyn, later Lila two sons came to stay, a little while, and she would tell my dad things like, I was staring at men in church, and he would beat me with a stint cord, and sometimes with a 2 by 4 wood, one day he beat me so bad that I ran out of the house, down the street, and was about to get in a random car, just to escape his beatings, my brothers ran down the street to catch me, I said to my brothers, no more ! no more !, I'm tired of them lying on me, and dad, he believes everything that they tell him about me, !! my brothers said don't worry Lynn, just take the beating this time!, I'm crying and saying no more ! no more, my brothers told me that my dad's wife and her sister, were just jealous of me and my dad relationship, but why ?/WHY I asked, I don't know Lynn, said my Oldest brother Franklin, but I'm going

to get us out of this house one day! And he did just that, one day he ran away, because when his girlfriend Jenelle, had called him at home on the phone, my stepmom Lila answered it, and told her not to call him anymore, because this was a holy house! And he couldn't have a girlfriend living under her roof, After that incident, my father beat him for the last time, my oldest brother left and got his own place, I was so happy for him, but also afraid, I stood and looked out the window, as he was running down the street, with no shoes on, no shirt on, just some cutoff jeans, but I also worried about how would he make it on his own, with no guidance, 17 years old, no money or food, no wear to live, me and my baby brother cried every night worrying about our Oldest brother Franklin, we often wondered where he was living, and would we ever see him again, . Finally one day I took a chance, and told one of my aunties, that I could trust, that my brother had ran away, because our stepmom didn't want him to have a girlfriend, she said she would talk to my dad, the (Bishop)about what was going on, and thank God she did, and he listen to her, I've had various counselors in my life, very religious parents that wouldn't let me join the military, which was something I really wanted to do after high school, I couldn't go to my high school prom, or be a cheerleader, all because of my parents Holy religious beliefs, and they didn't want me to wear the short skirts, so all I did as a young lady was go to school, church and back home, and never thought of having a boyfriend in high school, I have to say to my Aunt Bernice, thank you for speaking up for us 3 kids, when we couldn't

talk for ourselves. Back in 1977, I heard from my aunt bertha, that my first stepmother, Mrs. Jet had died of depression, my dad never even let me go back to visit her, even though I asked him several times, but he never listen, she had asked my dad several times also to bring me over to see her, he never did, and later her husband Mr. Wade passed, because he couldn't live without her, so he just drank himself to death and died of liver corrosion, she was a sweet lady, the best stepmom I ever had. I never got beat, or whipping by them,, When I used to hear people say that a Motherless child sees a hard time, I didn't know exactly what that meant, Now I know,!! I'm a living witness, and it's a true fact, While we were staying in our own house with Lila and her two sons, which she later became Mother Lila Smith, after marrying my father, dad gave her his church up in Atlanta on Glenwood AVE. She began to run that church, but people started leaving one by one, and my Dad was getting confused, and upset, asking what was wrong,? And why were the members leaving?, she replied I don't know, she thought people just didn't like her, but one of my aunt told my father, it was her Preaching and teaching, telling the women that they could not wear pants, makeup, or short skirts, to church. People were intimidated, so they started leaving one by one, soon after that, dad decided he just closed that church on Glenwood down. But he kept the ones in Jeffersonville, and Danville. My Dad was a man of good stature, and believed whatever the bible said, he's the only Preacher that I know who fasted 40 days, and 40 nights just like Christ, He began his 40 day fast at our

Danville church, at one of his members house, they lived in a double wide trailer home, I was about 15 years old then, I remember going in the room to see him, just before church that sunday, because for a week no one had saw my dad because he was fasting, only the couple that lived there, I was shocked when I saw him, because he didn't look like dad, he had lost about 30 lbs. and his face and body had shrunk, Everybody kept trying to get him to drink some juice, or eat a little something, He had enough strength to tell them no! that if Christ did it for 40 days and nights, he can do it also, so just leave him be!. So I'm dedicating this book to dad because He taught me onething, that is to be a strong women, and finish what you start, and to always read this Joshua 1;19 have I not commanded you? Be strong and courageous, do not be afraid, do not be dismayed, for the lord your god is with you wherever you go! I'm grown now I've been married for 8 years, and divorced three and have only one son Emanuel, named after his loving Father, that scripture has stuck with me for as long as I can remember, and yes my father was a kind hearted Man, who is greatly missed by all that knew him. He married me and my husband when I was only 19 and my husband was 26, we had a big church wedding at our Glenwood Church in Atlanta, before dad finally closed that church. He married several of my cousins, and siblings there also. Me and my husband had our difference, but we loved each other, the eight years we were together, seemed longer, when you are younger, we managed to raise a handsome son, that's married also. They are living in North Carolina, because he took a

job there as a web designer, when my son told me that he was moving out of TOWN I was overwhelmed with sadness,, because I had no one else I could depend on, because it has been me and him with each other, and depending on each other for support, He's my Pillow and back bone, that has always been with me through the good and the bad, if I desperately needed something, no matter where he was or who he was with, he would come to see about his Mother, well he moved and got a better designer job in North Carolina, I managed to keep my little apartment in Atlanta, but being alone was not a good feeling, and I missed him all the time, he still sent 300 a week to help me out whenever I needed it for rent or other bills, because I was in between jobs, after Southwest Hospital closed down where I was working, when he moved to North Carolina, his job helped him get a two bedroom apartment there, and he's doing well!, I'm so proud of him, I know his dad would be proud of him too, he has changed my life in so many ways, only a mother would know. My dad used to call me his black girl, when I was younger, after I got out on my own, Me and dad became closer, after we had our difference with each other, he began to see the real woman I became, I thought he didn't care about me when I was young, because he spent more time with the women and people in his church, than he did with his only daughter, I thought my dad hates me, because he didn't take up much time with me, when I was growing up,, me and my brothers were made to go to church even if we were sick, dad was very strict on us, he would let other people drive his car, loan them

money, but when I learned how to drive and needed the car, someone else always had it, he would buy them food, when me and my son needed food, if I called him he would always have an excuse, but god has brought me thru all of that, my child never went hungry, and we were never homeless, he didn't have the best of the best, but he was always neat and clean, I had a riches card that kept for years, just to buy my son a new suit for every Easter Sunday, that's the only card I remember that was always paid up, what my dad taught me was that when you don't know what to do, that's when you give it all to god, he will always bring you through . So that's what I learned to do, instead of depending on him a boyfriend or anybody else, because I had no mother to turn to, even though I never knew my mother, I knew that if she were here, she would help her only daughter, if we needed anything, but no one knew my situation, because I did what I had to do to keep me and my son together. My son didn't agree with some of the men I dated, my dad didn't either, I was kidnapped at gunpoint by the man I thought was my friend and lover, my child was home alone, sleeping while I was being kidnapped at gunpoint, when my father heard of that, he and my brothers, immediately came to the apartment and got my son, which was still sleeping upstairs, and they started looking all around the Atlanta South side for me, and that guy that had me driving him at gunpoint, I was told by my brothers that my dad had two guns, and was threaten to shoot and kill the guy when he saw him. Just so happen when we approached my house, the police had surrounded my place, and the first person I saw was my dad,!

standing like a gunman from an old western movie with 2 guns at his side, ready fire! The police yelled !!Sir! Sir !!!please, please put down the weapons!, we will take care of her, and this guy is going to jail for kidnapping.!! That's when I knew, that through it all, my dad really cared for his baby girl, Dad went home to glory in 1995, he finally apologize for all the wrong he had done to his three little children., and the way his family had treated us as children, He said he didn't know why they mistreated Us, or why the women in his life were so jealous of me and his relationship,, and why did they think every man that looked at me, wanted me, but I said to dad, I was only 13 or 14 ! a virgin and still fragile, never thought of having a boyfriend, how could they have treated a child so cruel, and to tell you I was pregnant, he replied daughter I don't know, I have no answer, but you will always be blessed because your mother left you in god's hand as an infant, no one can harm y"all now, just keep doing good, and try to live a Godly life, because god sees and knows everything. when you run into a bad situation, don't know what to do, look up to heaven, give it all to god, and he will bring you through! Dad has been gone for some years now, and my life, has a turned a 360 degree for the Best, and still turning, Oh but how I cried so many nights pacing and staring at the ceiling in my small 1 bedroom Apartment, asking God Why, Why put me through this pain of Grieving, now I'm here in this world without A mother and a father!. One thing I've learned growing up in the church, if you live for people's acceptance, you will die from their rejections, I tried so hard to fit in, to fill accepted, by my Dad and

his family, and the ones I thought love me, but being young, we were taught that you can't do anything, but obey your parents, or whomever is caring for you, we were told to go to church, not only on sundays, but anytime the church is having functions, or revivals, prayer meetings and so on. . . ., whether we wanted to go or not, we still obeyed our parents !, My father was the Bishop of 3 churches, he was a very strict and Religious man, that always discipline us, and totally believed in spare the rod spoil the child, This phrase comes from Proverbs 13;24, to me he was always serious about the bible and his church people, he was a peculiar man, by going to church so many years as a child, I've learned the LORD'S PRAYER, AND Serenity Prayer, some People may say that the serenity prayer was for AA, but it's for anybody going through life trying to overcome obstacles, I'll tell anyone that this simply prayer has gotten me over and beyond my tribulations, God grant me the Serenity, to accept the things I can-not change, the courage to change the things I can! and the wisdom to know the difference, .lord forgive my many errors that I made on yesterday, and let me try again today, to walk closer in thy way. I'm just thankful that when I did become pregnant, the man was bold enough to ask my dad for my hand, and my Dad Married us, in that Glenwood Ave Church, before he closed it down, and gave us a nice big Wedding, my Aunt Bernice and a friend of hers cooked all the food, and had a big watermelon zig zag display, that I loved and can never forget, but when I got Married I WAS SO GLAD TO BE AWAY FROM DADS RELIGIOUS WAYS, and his selfish wives, I FELT LIKE A FREE BIRD,

just waiting to fly away, but I never stopped Loving my father or his selfish wife's, My Heart, & Soul will not let me hate anybody, I guess God designed me that way. My Husband at the time, was 26 when my Dad married us, my Husband was a TALL DARK SKINNED MAN WEIGHED ABOUT 230 pounds, 6,2 in height, and a nice afro, it was so big it layed on top of his shoulders, I used to love to comb and just pick it out, our date of marriage was Aug 2, 1981, I've always said, there are not many real husbands like he was back in that day of time, in the late 70s early 80's, Back then my husband didn't want me to work, so I stayed home and took care our son, for the first couple of years, I took care the house, did my wife duties, which was to cook keep a clean house, and always kept my husband dinner ready for when he got home from work, he has always been a 18 wheeler truck driver, he traveled in and out of the Country, dropping off truck trailers, and in return, picking up empty trucks, bringing them back to Ga, or wherever the destination, One year in 1981 I took a trip with my husband to Florida to drop an empty trailer truck, and bring another 18 wheeler back loaded with children toys, we stopped at a rest stop, just before the Florida line, because he was tired of driving so long. And wanted to get a little sleep, I was given an allowance each week by my husband, when he got paid on Fridays, he was a very respectful man and loved to tell jokes, to make me laugh when he was home, we enjoyed our time together, never fusing our fighting, not only did he give me my allowance each week, but bought me and his baby boy, whatever we needed, He also paid every bill in

the house for 5 years, I was happy with my life,  and i still continue to go to my father's church when I could, until I was able to work and my son was able to walk and talk, and go to preschool, the only person we let kept our son was his mother, my mother in law, Johnnie Mae,  no one on my father's side of the family, or my family ever kept our son, we both agreed on that. We did have a Mexican couple that lived with us for a while, back in 1983 when we lived on MLK, my son was about 22 months old,  Mrs. Rita and her Husband Happy Gonzales, which are both deceased now,  they both spoke Spanish,  I never knew her husband happy real name, so my husband and everybody just called him happy,  they moved here to Atlanta,  from Richmond Texas, for a long time he and my husband worked together, at the Ga World Congress Center, before my husband started traveling over the road,  while the men worked, Me and Rita was home preparing our dinner, when I and My husband left for a while, she looked after my son,  he was walking and learning to talk, she was teaching him Spanish, and believe it or not he had learned some Spanish within 4 months!!, while she was there, me and my husband was shocked ! because he learned it in such short time, that's the only time they stayed with me and my husband,  until they finally got there own place, They moved out and things were back to normal, just me my husband and our son, my husband used to hide my son in a small basket, and fool me that he was stolen or missing, whenever I left the house, to go shopping, well as time went on,  we moved again and got a bigger place, my son was 5 years old,  when we moved to king Gardens

apts, I became good neighbors with a lady named Frances and her two daughters, that lived in the front of the complex, later me and frances began working together, at a temporary service, she was staying in the front, my brother Frank and his wife Wanda were living upstairs above me and my husband, One cold night in 1988 as me and my Family slept, I was awaken, with a knock at my door, my god ! who is knocking on my door this late at night, It was my brother and my cousin little Sammy, my brother had been shot in the back, but the bullet came out his side, he was still bandaged, and his crazy ass had just left the hospital,! before the doctors released him, he said he had called my cousin Sammy to pick him up from Grady Hospital, as I approached the door I could see he's outside sitting on the steps, smoking weed, talking with some guy and my cousin little Sammy, still wearing the bloodied bandaged, bullet wound not even healed yet, you know I asked the question any sister would ask, why in the world did you leave the hospital!?, before the doctors released you? Crazy boy! he replied he wanted to get back to his family and friends, I think he just wanted to get out and raise hell with his wife, and smoke weed, because that was part of his lifestyle, he even had me trying it, until one day before dad died, he found out that they were giving weed to me, and Dad chased my oldest brother all around the house with his gun, and told him he better not give me that mess again,, I was in my 20's, my baby brother Stevie was only 19, when I went to my brother Frank house, after about 5 years later, he had divorced his 1st wife Wanda, and was dating another chick name Corinthia, she was a

nice girl, short dark skinned kinda bow leg, medium shape, med dark black hair, she loved her beer, I witness her drinking a can of beer on our way to church one sunday afternoon!, I told her you better not let my dad see you drinking that beer,, because if you gotta drink alcohol before you go to church, and give god praise.! Then just don't go! I never understand why she did that, as I grew older and wiser, I realized that she had not been in our church long enough to know that was wrong,! and my brother said that she was so naive, she just didn't know any better, because no one had ever told her that it was wrong, to drink alcohol before going to church, my reply to him was, you are the Oldest, and the preacher's son, you should tell her that's wrong! yes I did tell her that was wrong, but I can't judge her, because we all young, and doing wrong going to church, I told her please try not to drink alcohol, before coming to church, because my dad would smell it, and if he ever caught you it will be devastating, but we all were naive, & young, so that statement was ignored by her, she continued to drink, until my dad told her that he better not catch her with a beer in her hand, or near her mouth, if he did he would make her eat it,!, One evening, when i visited her at my brother house in decatur, they were always drinking and smoking, I liked to drink my cella lambrusco wine, so on friday which was payday for my brothers, and my husband, my brothers were always glad to see me come over, my oldest brother, would make it his business to buy me a 5th of Cella Lambrusco Red Wine on payday, that friday I meet him at his house, and my baby brother was there also,, we did not know that my dad the Preacher,

was coming over for whatever reason, so as we all were in the house drinking and smoking my brother Frank just happen to be looking out the window and saw my dad's car pull up!, he started screaming and yelling!! dads outside y'all,! dads outside! Spray, and give me more spray before he comes in here!!, I was excited to see dad, but they told me to stay in the house, and go to the back room, go go get outta here Lynn! because they knew i would be a dead giveaway with me silly laughing, at everything and everybody, and they didn't want my dad to see me, so as I got up to go in the back of the house, I could hear my dad outside asking ?, is Linda in there? where's my black gal? I wanna see my black Gal, he used to call me, I was scared straight,! so just I turned to see where he was, and open the screened door by accident, as I was trying to get back in the door, I fell on my knees, and started laughing, everyone was yelling at me, Lynn! Lynn get back to the back, we don't want dad to see you,!! or know that you are over here, please ! get in the back room!, but I was so excited and intoxicated that I stumbled and fell out the Screen door, on to the steps,! I know my dad was watching me, I tried so hard to catch my balance, before rolling all the way down the hill, and landed near his foot, he was standing up against his car, this big blue Lincoln, he stood over me and looking up at my brothers, in anger, asking them, what did y'all do? And why did y'all give her that stuff,! Didn't I tell y'all not to give her that mess!! they replied, dad we didn't give her anything!!, dad replied yes yall did, and I'm gonna beat you and Stevie butt when I catch you !, my brothers started running back towards the house laughing, my dad

replied yall should not have gotten her drunk!, she's my baby girl!, Even though I just got married, and out of his house, he still called me his baby girl, my son is 30 now, and I still call him my baby boy, it's a family thing I guess, so after that incident, I never went over there house again, smoking and drinking, I was ashamed that my dad the Pastor of our church, had to see me like that, he had always preached, that whatever is done in the dark, shall come to the light!, And I am a living witness to that, But it was all part of growing up, as for myself that has happen to me twice in my life back then, and 2010 when I was going through trying to find a job and bills were sky high, dad was deceased, My only oldest brother in jail, child all grown up, and moved away, so I felt like I was all alone, every time I got stressed, started crying, about lord I need a job, 48 and out of work is no laughing matter, so I turned to alcohol as a comfort, not thinking clearly, using up money that I could have been saving to pay on bills, instead I would drink & and try not to think about my problems, money would come in my hands, if it wasn't enough to pay all my bills, I would be depressed and stressed for days, but when I lost several good jobs,, my son and his wife, found out about how I didn't even get the job, that's when I really woke up, I wanted to die and never face life again! but so many celebrities have drowned in their own sorrows and didn't make it back to reality, but I remember dad saying, when you are all out of answers, and no one to turn to, just give it all to god, and he will bring you through! So again whatever we're doing wrong, it's hurting ourselves, and also hurting others, we just don't see it

at that moment, so this time I'm doing it the right way, if I don't have enough money, to pay all the bills, or get what I need, I've learned how to save, save and put away for the next day. Why ? was I a victim of substance abuse anyway, It was my problem, a disease a sickness, that no-one could help me, but god and prayers,, I can see now, how much better my life and mind is without clutter, I have a testimony every day, not only on sundays, that yes! prayer does change people, and situations, My baby brother Stevie can also be witness to that, because 20 years ago so many people in our family, said that his baby boy, Elijah was not his son, only because he looked like a white baby when he was born, some family members said that his wife was cheating on him with a whiteman, and that he should leave her, and even my dad told her in a kidding manner, that he wouldn't have neither one of them boys as a husband, talking about his own 2 sons, my baby brother Stevie is just like my father, even the same height, and muscular build, with hazel eyes, but no matter what other people said about him and his wife Vernita she didn't listen to all that negative talking, she stayed true, right there with her husband, Even when he didn't have a job, through the good and the bad just like the marriage vows say, for better or worse, whether he was working, cheating or not, who's to say? or judge him, no one but he & god was there if it ever happen, they have been together now for 25 years,! Steve has been on the same job for 16 years, and their son Elijah is a split image of the both of them, their son is 15 now, and they are buying a lovely home in jonesboro ga, so you see no matter what others

may say or do, your life is still up to you! I'm still saving money here and there, and since I've started, I don't want to stop until I see 6 FIGURES or more in my accounts, It's a habit I love now, I won't stop,  because I have a GRANDBABY ON THE WAY! This grandma I'm gonna make sure he has everything a child needs, just as I did when his father was a child,  I did the very best I knew how for my only son, change comes with maturity,  I never knew that saving could become addictive, like bad habits, especially if you have a steady job, my dad taught me about wisdom of age, when you get my age you will understand, he was right, now I'm passed his age,  in my late 30s but finally I understand, don't let the littleness of others, bring out the littleness in you. A mirror reflects a woman's face, but what she's really like, is shown by the kinda friends she chooses. And for years, and years I choose the wrong friends, well I thought they were my friends, Now I know from experience that they were not my real friends, they were just interested in what I had,  or what I could give them,  I just wanted to fit in the crowd,  I always worried about what other people thought of me,  my friends and family especially my Father (Bishop), everyone used to call him,  I was Very self-conscious,  and it kept me feeling sorrow for myself, so I tried to fit into their world, But as a child it was very hard because my father was making us be these Holy Ghost kids, that we knew nothing about, I'm in my first year of high school and was made to wear this little bunet on my head everyday as a head covering,  skirts below my knees, and other kids would laugh because they didn't understand our

religion, and why me a young girl in high school, was made to wear those things, but as long as I was under my fathers, roof I had to go by his rules, or get beat by him, So after I changed that dark area of my life, got away from dads house, and his religious Holy rules, I changed my life forever, But once out of his house I never forgot God, I had to clean up what I messed up! when I was weak, in mind and spirit, I cried and ask god to give me strength and a second chance,, when I messed up, he forgave me. When I wanted to go left, he kept me on the right path, after I fell on my knees and cried out to him so many lonely nights, I'm all out of answers, don't know what to do, so I'm giving it all to YOU!, Like a child beginning to walk, I had to restart my goals, restart my life, it doesn't take a new year, to make a new start ! and weigh every situation as it arises, That's why to me, it's important to say the serenity prayer daily, because there will be some things in life, that you and I cannot change, just ask god to give you wisdom, if it's something you don't know if it's the right decision or not!... In this life we can't survive without asking for advice !! be careful how you live, you maybe the only bible some people read! So I pray for purity, unselfishness, I can't forget these things I was taught living in the holy house with my father, BISHOP, and a stepmother, I still read the bible daily, well now with the new technology, I can have the bible read to me! I try to keep away from people who belittle my ambitions, small people with No self-discipline will do that, but really good and honest people, make you feel that you can be good, and become a better person. Be kind to one another, tenderhearted,

forgiving one another, even as God has forgiven Us <. Ephesians 4;32. Some things happen in my past youth, I ran away from home at 16, staying with other people I did not even know,  I was raped while away from home,  my family Mistreated me as a child sometimes, I didn't have nice clothes or other things like my other cousin had,  I went without food sometimes,  because I didn't have a job, too young to work,  and no money,  so I lived with people just to have a place to sleep,  but I survived and overcame all my obstacles, the best way a motherless child could. All Because I wanted to get out of that holy house, god is close to the brokenhearted, my heart was broken, so many times as a child, and I had no one I could turn to, after I ran away from home,  but Matt 19 :14 says suffer little children, ,  to come unto me, when I learned god had took my mother at age 24, why ?why? was always the question in my mind,  why my mother,! I was beaten by a jealous boyfriend, that tried to kill me just because I gave another schoolmate a ride home,  I was Beaten by my father, because someone in our family told him I was pregnant,  at age 13, I knew nothing about sex, I was still a Virgin,  but if I had my mother to talk to or run to ask her advice,  some of those things that happen to me, could have been avoided!,  But I was self -taught and have learned to forgive, as Christ forgave those who beat him, because if not, it's like digging in an open sore, that wound never heal, Meaning your heart will never heal of the pain and hurt, if you keep picking and aggravating that sore, dwelling on the past, but after letting go, and letting god take control of my life, I try my best to

forget about it, that's why I'm writing about it, and talking about it, because that was a situation, that I could not change! or control, Our life reflects on the book of psalm, I will lie down, and sleep in peace; for you alone, O Lord, make me lie down in safety, Psalm 13;6. Always keep in touch with God, and he will keep in-touch with you! Bless me heavenly father, forgive my erring ways, and put purpose in my days, I waited patiently for god to help me; because as a little girl walking on the streets, not knowing what to do or where to go, God was my only hope, then he listened and heard my cry. Avoid self-preoccupation, because there will be many who need the assistance, and advice that only you can offer. One thing I did learn in dads teaching, and preaching. (The Lord is near to the brokenhearted, and saves the crushed in spirit, read it for yourself in psalms 34;18.) It doesn't take a new year, to make a new start, it only takes deep desire, and try with all your Heart!!, I ask god daily to forgive my many errors, because I know that no day is too dark, no burden too great, that god and his love cannot penetrate. Lord as I travel this road alone today, whatever confronts me, lead & protect me every step of life's way! TLC, Tender Loving Caring, tell your story, live your passion, change your world. We all have a story to tell, we all have a purpose in this life, and a mission to complete, in order to get where we want to be, don't just live your life for others, but live the way you think is best for you, always strive for the best, never just settle for anything. God wants us to have the best of all in his world, so change your world, live a godly life, everything is done for a reason, My mother left me here on this

earth, as a 13 month old baby girl, and I cried day and night asking GOD why! WHY my Mother !? for a reason that only god knows,, I ask myself is this my season? it's time for me to be on my mission, change start with a decision, nothing is by accident, not even our problems, our problems can be solved, In life we do what we gotta do, until we can progress, then do what we wanna do! that's a decision for a purpose, we can't change the world, until you change yourself,. I'll have a testimony for the rest of my LIFE, to tell the next person, Or the next young motherless child, of how I've completed my mission, and told my life story, because no one can tell it, like I can! Our parents can only give us good advice, or put us on the right paths, but the final forming of a person's true character,! lies in their own hands, the final decision is Ours. But I always take pride in how far I have come, and have faith in how far I can go! There is no giant steps in persistence, but a lot of little steps, a little here, little there, but I will get there, if I set my goals, and focus on them, you have to believe in yourself, and have more self-control, which is something I'm working on daily, when nobody else believe in me, I need to be strong & positive, and have self-motivation so that nothing can disturb MY inner peace ! pain is temporary. . . . I know it first hand, it may seem forever, but if we don't think about it, it will soon ease away. If we are ashamed of asking for help, like I was as a child, then we are ashamed of learning, It's like in high school, our teachers opened their doors, but we had to enter our classroom ourselves. A three year old baby girl survived an earthquake, an earthquake happen at the time of

Jesus death, Matt 27, that three year old baby girl, survived for three days, no food no water, when pulled out from under brick and rubbish, she did not even cry! true fact, that Jesus does love the little children,! We are all different, we may have different religions, different languages, different colored skin, but we all have the same One God!. You may be disappointed, if you fail in something, whatever it maybe, but you are doomed, if you don't keep trying to perfect it., the harder you work, the better your success, I know the road to success runs uphill! that's the way I'm traveling, for the rest of my days, and there's still some healing needs to be done in my life>I've learned that in order to gain or proceed in this life, we have to let go whatever is stopping us, whatever is keeping us BACK! games can't be won unless they are played, and prayers cannot be answered, If not prayed! It may be a love one, an acquaintances,, or a family member, or just a dead end job, but whatever the case may be, don't let it stop you from going forth, we all have excuses, I had plenty excuses when I was young, my dad ask me one day before getting a whipping, why did you do that? he asked me again, again, the only answer I had was, the devil made me do it!, I'm sorry daddy,! I'm sorry daddy, but the devil made me do it, that's no excuse to him, even though I gave him my excuse, my reason, he still whip my butt!, so I learned that excuses does not work all the time, you may get buy for now, but you won't get ahead, staying in the same old place, or position, you have to be on a mission to better yourself, staying in the same circle is not good! If the people in your circle are not trying to get ahead, and always

complaining, then get out that circle, if you're talking about getting your own business,, and the people in your circle are saying, you shouldn't, because you can't afford it, definitely get out that circle, because in this life, you get what you put in. If you never put in, or invest in something, then you can't expect to receive anything, you will be left standing waiting on nothing. Even if you don't see your Blessing, that's called faith, declare it, & claim it!. I have discovered my passion, I'm going to prepare my life for a change, I'm laying out my goals, and carrying them out to the end, even if it takes me a couple of months, or years, Or even a lifetime, it may take some people less, or more, because I can't finish, if I don't get started, so whatever your plans are, carry them out, and try not to let that bad circle of people stop you from moving forward to the next level in your life. This is my plan, now I'm in the second chapter of my life, preparing for the end. I have a grand baby on the way, and I really want to be able to talk to him or her, and tell them some good and sad stories, they would not believe the struggle that grandma has come over such huge mountains, By then I hope to be on a smooth road, relaxed, and confident, and able to love & care, and give them all my attention, good advice, and putting them on the right paths at an early age, that's important to me. Because that's one thing I didn't have as a young child growing up, a mothers Love and guidance, and someone to teach me about love and respecting others, I learned all about respect, and the love of god, when I started staying with my religious Father, I want to help raise my grandkids, teach them that you have to earn respect, by showing it,

and giving it first, you have to always better yourself, and move up, never stay in the same old situation, I can't teach them about climbing, and going over a mountain, unless I've tried it first, I can't tell them that their feelings won't be hurt, but the pain will ease, and go away, If I haven't had my feelings hurt, or lost my best friend, my father and a mother, if It didn't happen to me first, how I went through the pain and sorrow,  How could I tell them about my sorrow and grief,  if I never had to grief through the good and the bad, it's my story and testimony to tell them the truth, no one can speak about my life, but the source. *I ju*st hope that in their little hearts, they understand that in this life you have to earn whatever you want, even if it's more allowance, more toys, a better car,  you still have to earn it by showing your gratitude, that you appreciate what you have now, always say please and thank you, to the person you're receiving it from, that's makes you feel good about yourself, and it makes you a good person of character, then you can move forward, to receiving much better blessings, and bigger things, or whatever it is that you want in life, just always respect yourself, and show respect to others especially your Seniors, and your Mother and Father, Even if they don't show it to you, that's makes you the bigger, and better person! You can't be dishonest, just because your friend is being dishonest, you have to be the better person and walk away from that environment, and seek other honest friends, and co-workers. Don't get the blame for someone else mistake or wrong doings, just because you are with them, That's why daily you need wisdom and knowledge, to know

right from wrong! Grandma is to help teach you, and help you understand, that no one cares for you, like your Mother and Father, so always respect them, you are here because of them, and the love and respect they have for each other. Your father is a great dad, he has worked most all of his life, Just like his father did, he got his first job at the age of 14, at a Winn Dixie grocery store, pushing buggies, in the scorching hot sun, and was giving me, his mother, just about all of his hard earned money, because he knew that I only had a part time job, and was getting AFDC at that time, he cared for my well-being, even though I was on state assistance receiving a little money, he always worried about me, I should have been more compassionate, about taking money from him, I feel so ashamed of myself as a parent now as I look back, because he's the one that worked so hard in the hot sun, just to make that little min wage paycheck each week, he even got mugged once, coming home from that 6.25 an hour job, when he knocked on the door and I opened it, all my eyes could see!! Was the blood running down his face, and chest! I went into a panic mode, Oh my god!!! OH MY GOD !! was all I could say, and pulled him into the house and locked the door !, because I didn't know whether the person or people was still behind him, I called the ambulance, and the police, the Ambulance rushed him to southwest hospital, where he got 10 stitches in the back of his head, from where he was hit with the butt of a gun, I had worked at Southwest hospital for 6 years as a Security Guard/ transportation Driver, so all Doctors and Nurses there knew me, and gave my son the best care, he later told me

how he was mugged, as he was walking home that night from work, I knew he got off at 10;00pm, I was wondering why it was taking him so long to get home, it was 11;00pm <I even called the store to see where he was, the cashier Antonette, which was one of his friends that knew me, and she said Ms. Johnson he should be on his way home, once my son arrived home, he told me as he was walking on the sidewalk, he heard these guys behind him, talking about robbing someone, so he crossed the street, they came across the street also, and pushed him in these thick bushes, and hit him in the back of his head with a gun, and made him lay down on the railroad tracks, where there were other people laying also, that they were robbing, they took his wallet, and the word organizer reader, that I just bought him, The next week his wallet was found in the Winn Dixie parking lot, the police called me two weeks later and told me that it was two brothers that was robbing people, in the MLK area, at that time we were staying on Harlan Rd, off of MLK, the Police told me, they both were shot and killed by a home owner, they were trying to break in his house, my son had been through so much that year that's why I didn't, want to take any money from him, but that was a learning and teaching process for him and me, we learned from each other, we over came our obstacle, he has always been taught, to love and be obedient, and respect your Mother and father, no matter what the situation or problem is, whenever I asked him for something, he never told me no, finally one day when he was 16, he told me mom,! I can't maintain my girlfriend, with you taking my money!, He was right,

I felt so bad that I cried for days, and felt so ashamed but no one knew the hurt I felt, I apologized to my son, but I still felt small as a parent, because I realized that I was hurting my only son, but I was listening to a sorry man, that I had let put his hands on my son for the last time, at that time, he was my 2nd husband, asking me to get money from my son, I felt like an ant!. that needed to be stomped!, and I never wanted to come out of hiding!. I asked god to remove me from that man and that situation, forgive me for hurting my only child, but guess who God sent as my Refuge helper, that I didn't know was already there, to bail me out of an abusive situation, my own son came up with a 250.00 deposit for our next apartment, My son came home from high school, after playing football one day and said mama, don't worry, we will get away from this situation, I don't know who or where he got the money from, all I can say is, thank you, thank you Lord! for saving us, I do believe he had help from his girlfriend parents, I will never know, but they never judged me, or belittled my lifestyle, but I knew God was helping me and my son to get away from where we were, and away from the anguish I was putting on him, and myself, , I constantly asked my son to forgive me again, before I could ask god to forgive me, because I thought god was punishing me for my wrongdoing, but my son came to me one day and said no moma, god is not punishing you, And I love you no matter what, I was young and I felt like I should have been locked away, for putting him through that at such young age, But I raised him to love be a respectful, & Honest young man, and we have always been there

for each other, no matter what situation, he played football at Mays High, and if he missed the school bus, he would walk to school, we lived about 2 miles from his school, but he was determined to go, then he went on to finish college at the art Institute of Atlanta, but now I think that god has punished me in so many other ways, It will take me another book to explain it to you, I'm just merely saying, that you have to be honest with yourself, before you can be honest with others. Because God sees everything, and knows everything before it's done! So to move forward to the next level in your life, remember to respect your parents, and grandparents, which are smart and intelligent people, to my grandkids when you grow up, this is a story you can share with you kids, that all parents are not perfect people, we make mistakes, but I assure you, that we are striving everyday, to be better in whatever we are doing in life! and whatever they are trying to accomplish. Always strive to be a better person. Now that I've told you a little about my past, I'm gonna leave it there, in the PAST!, because all of that is dead to me now, I'm moving forward to the future, a renewed me, (2nd CHAPTER) Let me tell you about my life as a live-In caregiver, and how it has changed my life for the better, I became a nurse's aid in 1993, and I never thought that I would someday, be traveling, as a live-in caregiver, Because caring for others is a passion for me, It all started in 2006, when Southwest hospital closed, and it seems that i could never find a steady job, Id work 3, 6 months, or even a year, here and there, but something would always go wrong, and its last in, and first out the door, so I

kept putting in applications at least 15 or 20 online each week, as a caregiver, or live-in Aide, and finally, I saw where I could go to Connecticut, and work as a live-in caregiver, I called them, and they pulled my resume, and noticed I had over 15 years of experience in healthcare, they asked when could I start, because they were in big demands, for experienced CNA aides, I said I could start right away, because my husband was deceased, and my only son had just moved out of town to North Carolina, so I had nothing holding me back, they paid for me a greyhound ticket, and said they had an apartment above their office, for me to live, until I go out on my new case, a driver from the company would pick me up and take me to the clients home, and also pick me up when the case is over or when I needed a break or vacation, I said yes!! That sounds Great, so I called my son and asked him for about 60 dollars just to get me some food and traveling expenses, I was just offered a job out of town!, he said you got the job Mom that's good! I said yes but it's a thousand miles away from here, he ask me are you going to take it? I said of course I am, my son replied I'm so happy for you mama, well now you don't have to be at the house by yourself worrying all the time, when he came to Atlanta that weekend, he brought the money to me, I could always depend on my son before I would any man, that's why I say I can't, and I won't let another man come between me and my Child ever again, Like I did when he was small, and I was younger, because it's has been me and him through everything, good and bad, and we always gave each other the utmost respect, I got the ticket in the mail the next

week, and I got on greyhound, and I was picked up from the bus station, Once I arrived in Connecticut just as the Company had said, and taken to the office apartment, and I've been with them ever since, I didn't know that they would be sending me all over to different parts of the states, From Stratford Connecticut, Massachusetts to New England Martha's Vineyard, and all in between, but I love it because you get travel, meet all types of people, and see how other people live, the first client I was assigned, was a Catholic lady, her name was Marge, and she was 89, born July 31, 1927. After I began living with Ms. Marge, I learned she did not like lights on after 8:00 pm, I lived at the Atria Assisted living with her from Jan 8, 2015-thru August 28, 2015, it was only a 1 bedroom apartment, of course I slept in the living room on an Air Mattress, because she had a love seat, and she told me that it was over 50 years old, I could tell, because I could not believe what I was seeing, so I took pictures, and sent them to my employer, she had duck tape on every corner of that loveseat, and when you sat on it, the cushions were so rotten, that the particles, were coming out on your clothes, every time I got up off that love seat, I was constantly brushing stuff off of my pants, which was so annoying, she had no kids, or living relatives that could come and take her to buy a new couch. So I asked my job could I take her, and explained to them that she has duct tape all on the sofa where I'm supposed to sit, they wanted to know how would we get there and back, I told them we would get dropped out at Bob's Furniture store, by the facility driver, she told them that she would pay for a

cab for us to get back. I agreed to pay half of the cab fare coming back, because it made no sense for her to live like that, when she had the money, but no would come and take her around, so I offered to help her, since i would be living there also, So on March 26, 2015, it was a rainy day, the van from Atria took us to bobs furniture, and dropped us off, she picked out a new couch, and paid for it that day, and we caught a cab back, March 31, 2015 at 1;45 pm it was delivered, and she was so happy!, she said no one has ever helped her do anything, she told me she had asked her lawyer, which was her power of attorney, and he told her that he was going out of town, and for her to ask one of the girls that worked for him in the office, well she did ask one of them, and the lady told her that she had a small car, and she was not able to take her, Marge was also wearing old clothes from the late 40s or earlier, and she was a beautiful lady, she told me, she grew up a catholic, and went to an all girls catholic school, she was about 125 pounds, shaped nicely, and never even been married, she stated that, she dated a guy when she was in her early 30s, he wanted to get married and she didn't, because she knew that he wanted to have kids, and she didn't want any children, she told me she broke up with him, because she refused to have kids for him, the next month as we got to know each other better, I noticed she was wearing the same stirrup pants, and spotted blouses, I could hear the Nurse, and aides always whispering about how Nice looking she was, but her clothes were outdated, the next week, I could not tell her they were talking about her clothes, so I asked her? would she like

some new pants ?, and if so, I could order her some new clothes, but I would have to get it cleared, through my office first, because the people there at her facility, wasn't very helpful at all, when it came to her personal items, they would always ask me the question ? why didn't she buy her something better, well I asked Ms. Marge about that, because one morning as I was getting her a change of clothes, out of her small closet, I noticed that she only had about 6 complete outfits, and most of her blouses, had oily food stains, so on laundry day I concentrated on trying to remove all the stains, from her tops, but did not succeed, so finally I go up the nerve to just ask her why she never bought new clothing, well I knew she didn't drive, because she told me that she never even had a license, but the facility has outings each week, to walmart, the dollar store, and target, but she stated to me that she never thought about it, because growing up being Catholic, they wore the same thing everyday, she attended catholic school from 2nd grade to college, when she finished college she became a Nun, and worked at the local hospital as a Nurse, and don't remember even buying new clothes, because she always wore a uniform, therefore she just wore what she had, I didn't like the fact, some of the ladies at that facility talking about her, because once you got to know Ms. Marge, she was a very polite, and quiet Lady that did not like to much company around, and would use daylight wisly to read her books, because when the sun went down she would cut off all the lights at 8;00 pm every night and WENT to bed at 8;30pm, the following week I asked Ms. Marge would she like to order her some new

clothes from blair, only because I would see her looking through that catalog everyday, and she could look at them on my computer to see how she liked them, before we placed the order, she said that would be nice, so I order the first pair pants and a rose colored Blouse, just to see if she would like it, and paid for them with my card, that was a little gift from me to her, she was so happy when the pants and blouse arrived, I assisted her with putting them on, and she was just smiling, saying they were her color, oh my Gosh this is my color!, and how did you know my favorite color, she asked me? I didn't know, i just thought they would look nice with your completion, she wanted me to order her more so we sat down to order her about 5 more new outfits, when her clothes arrived in about two weeks, I began to dress her in different outfits, when I would escort her down for lunch and dinner in the Afternoons, the staff and people in the dining room at the facility was like wow,! One of the aides that gives her daily Medicine, said Marge you've had at least 8 aides here to care for you, and neither one of them, has bought you anything, then, the Aide asked Marge, are you related to her? Marge replied No, she's just my New Caregiver, the next day when I took her down to the dining room for lunch, everybody was staring, and saying oh oh, is that Marge? They asked, I heard someone say Marge you have a good caregiver Now! you both look very nice!! Then out of the corner of my eye I could see and hear some of her lady friends whispering amongst themselves, I knew Ms. Marge could have done more for herself, Only if she had just the right helper, and a little self-motivation, so

I feel that I was in the right place at the right time, the next month on April 14, which is my Dad's Birthday, also my Nephew Elijah birthday, a Virus broke out in the facility, and several people were getting sick, stomach aches, diarrhea, vomiting with a fever, as a result when I washed my hair that weekend, my hair came out on the sides, and top, I was hysterical!, My client Marge was having diarrhea, and staying in the bathroom a lot, I called my baby brother Stevie, (Minister Clark) back in Atlanta crying hysteria!!! giving him the address of where I was working, just in case, something else were to happen to me, he told me to stop crying, and that everything would be alright, he also started praying for me as I could not stop crying, I'm a thousand miles from home, and I don't know anyone up here!, I'm just up here working trying to make a living for myself, I told him a virus had broke out in this Facility and my hair continues to fall out !, what am I going to do!, all my baby brother Stevie could say was Lynn, Lynn please stop crying please, let's pray, let's pray together over the phone, I felt a little better, after HE and I had prayed and talked, the next Morning, the Manager of the facility, came around to everyone's room and said to stay in our rooms, because a bug was going around, they're trying to figure out where it came from, because about 20-25 people were affected, and of course Me and Marge were in that 25, she said the health department, would be coming to everybody's room, in a couple of days, to ask what are their illness, and not to go to the dining room for meals,, and do NOT go in the hallways, our meals would be delivered three times a day, by the chef, and

the kitchen staff, they will have on mask and special clothing, they told us that no one will be coming in or go out of the Atria, because it's being quarantined until further notice from the health department, and they would deliver the menus daily, circle what we want for lunch and dinner, then slide it back under the door, the Kitchen staff would come around to each floor and pick them up, the following morning a knock was at the door, I answer it, the women on the other side said Health Department, we had just finished our morning coffee, and was still waiting for our breakfast to be delivered, I opened the door slowly to let the woman in, and she began to ask us questions, about how we were feeling, and did we think it was the food, Me and Marge looked at each other, and Marge said well that's all I do around here is eat and sleep, i asked her, could it be the water? Because when I washed my hair last night the top and sides of my HAIR just started falling out, !! and I'm still scared of this, because no one knows what it is, Please, please, can you all do something quick, we have a lot of Seniors in here that have weak immune systems, and their fragile bodies cannot take all this, The women from the health Department said, well it could be a food virus, but were looking into several things, Please inform your family, that no One can come into the Atria to visit or leave the building, some people will be coming to clean the dining rooms, shampoo all the floors, But they will be wearing special clothing and shoes, we will keep in touch with all the Residents and the Owners of Atria, we followed those instructions for two weeks, over the next several weeks my hair began to grow

back, Everyone staying out of the halls, and stayed in their Own Rooms, on friday April 24, a flyer was slid under our door, saying Welcome Back Residents!!!, the dining room, Activity Room, theater, and the salon are now open, all staff Nurse Aides, and Residents can return to normal activity, the letter also stated that Atria quickly implemented all necessary precautions to eradicate the GI Bug, that visited the community since April 14, and thanks for everyone cooperating, so I continued to live there for 8 months with Ms. Marge being her caretaker, and several weeks later, I was so happy when it was time for me to take my two weeks vacation, when that time came I went home to Atlanta Ga, when I returned to Connecticut, from my two week stay in Atlanta, i was put on a new case, the company had sent someone else, to care for Marge, and stated that they needed me on a new case in Oxford Connecticut, I didn't mind at all, being put on another Case, I didn't want to keep staying at the Atria, because of the previous Virus That had broken Out, My Lady Marge was doing just fine with another Aide also, I called to check on her once i got settled with my new Clients, which was an Italian family, a husband and wife, Marge told me she missed me but she was doing good, my New Client was the husband, Mr. Ralph, he was born September 14,1938, had a partial amputation left foot, and a quarter size open sore on the right foot, and I learned later that he has stage 4 colon cancer, Ralph had one daughter who introduced me to her father, she wept as she began to explain to me his pass, pain and condition, she also handled all of his bills, medical, and doctor appointments,

she also had two brothers, one was deceased, the oldest son was a police officer of Oxford CT,, I often wondered why, the wife would not care for her disabled husbands wound, because the bible says Ephesians 5;22 for wives to submit themselves to their husband, love one another in sickness and health, until death do us part, a wife should care for her husband especially if he's ill, they had been married for over 40 years, as i began living there, i found out why she didn't want to care for him, or change the bandages on his foot, he had the wound care nurses coming in twice a week, they showed me how to care for his wound, and they showed his wife also, but she would not change the dressing for him, I could be in my room down the hall sometimes, after I had finished cooking supper, and cleaning the kitchen, I could hear her tell him several times to call me, she would do some simple things for him, like get him a soda, or fix him a snack, or a lunch if he had a doctor's appointment, but any and everything else was left for me to do the rest, because his wife knew I was getting paid to care for him, that's why I was there, they had a beautiful home in Oxford Connecticut, it snowed off and on through the 7 months i was there, caring for Mr. Ralph from April 28 to November 14, 2014, his wife loved to gamble at mohegan sun's whenever she got a chance to go with her son, he was the Oxford Police Officer, Married and his wife was a Nurse that worked in the Maternity Ward, at the Connecticut Hospital, she had asked me to come alone also, I said yes because this was my first time going to the Mohegan Sun< I was excited that she asked me to come alone! Her son the police

officer, would always be the one to take us, her daughter never went with us to Mohegan Sun Casino, we only went every other Friday it was an hour Drive from there home in Oxford Connecticut, I was told by their daughter in their younger days the Husband and wife both were heavy drinkers, but when her Father became ill, with colon cancer, and a diabetic, he was told by his doctors, to stop drinking, and the wife continue to drink, but he continued, as a result, his diabetes became worse, and his left foot was amputated, due to the diabetes, also his cancer progressed to stage 4 colon cancer, but he still continued to drink, but not as heavy, he and his wife augured all the time about something, when I wasn't attending to him, I would stay in my room and close the door, but even with my door closed, I could still hear them arguing, I went on vacation for Christmas in 2014, and told them I would be back in two weeks, and another nurse would come in and relieve me, before I left, I told the wife that I could show her a simpler way to clean and dress her husband heel wound, that would eliminate odors, but she seemed uninterested, and stated that his wound care nurse, would be still coming, so I left that weekend and stayed two weeks at home in Atlanta with my family, his daughter called me and said that i don't have to come back because he had a pacemaker put in Feb, a couple days after I left, and he died a week later, he used tell me he just wanted to die, because he didn't like the fact that me and other people had to take of care of him, and his wife of 40 years don't love him anymore, I told him please don't talk like that, because you have a daughter that loves you very

much, and I'm sure your wife still loves you too, she and your daughter are reason I'm here, to give you the best care possible!, so you should look forward to living each day, because it will get better, When I returned on February 16, I was assigned another case in Stoneham Massachusetts, her name was Mrs. Nancy she was 89, born Feb 15, 1927 and weighed 100 pounds, light gray hair, with a layer shortcut style, very sweet Italian lady, I worked there from February 2015-Feb 17, 2016 which is my baby brother birthday, once I started this case, Mrs. Nancy Daughter informed me that her mother illness has left her prone to infection, even with a simple cold, it could develop into pneumonia, so I had to make sure that she kept her coat on, each time we took our daily walks outside, which was twice a day, once outside, and once up and down the hallway of her building, it snowed or rained every other day that I was there, when I came there to work as her live in Caregiver, she had just celebrated her 89th birthday, it was a two bedroom retirement facility located in Stoneham Mass, she had one daughter that did everything for her, all the food shopping, driving her to all of her appointments, she even took her Mother to her husband's grave every Saturday afternoon, he loved reese's cup, and donuts, so the daughter would bring a pack of reese's cup and a donut, for her mother to put on her husband headstone, even though the critters would eat it, they would replace it the next saturday when she visited his grave, I had never seen anyone do this before, whether it was a rainy, or snowy day, her daughter would come and take her Mother to visit her husband and youngest

daughter grave every Saturday! my dad passed almost 10 years ago at age 54 with lung cancer, and I only visited him on Father's day, but i never visited his grave once a month, after the first time visiting him on Father's day, it was just to overwhelming for me, but I have an Auntie Bernice, that loves to visit the grave sites, even though she's in her 80s now, she still can remember where everyone in our family is buried! Which is amazing to me because after 20 years, I could not remember where my own father the pastor was buried! this Italian family visited the husband and her daughter grave every saturday, No matter what! the Mother had told me, the deceased daughter favorite color was yellow, so every year on the deceased daughter's birthday, they would buy a fresh yellow rose, to put on her headstone and would leave a card saying happy birthday we love you, I thought this was a wonderful thing to do for your loved one, today is Dec 24, Christmas eve day, her daughter Joann has invited us to her home for Christmas dinner, and they will be exchanging gifts, I told her daughter that I have not purchased a gift, she said not to worry, that she has gifts for me and her mother to participate in the giveaway, her daughter had prepared shrimp with red sauce, and all types of seafood, all marinated and cooked in red sauce, which is what I call marinara sauce, while we were there about 30 of her friends came and they began playing a game and exchanging gifts, I won 3 bottles of wine, and 50 dollars, someone else won the blacket and picture, that she had bought for me to put in the game, Me and her mother enjoyed ourselves while at her daughter's house, I had never heard of a

limoncello Italian wine, the wine was a bright yellow I was so excited to receive that, because I knew in Atlanta we had never heard of such wine, I was anxious to get it home, so I could try it, when her daughter drove us back to her mother's retirement home, Once we got into the house I noticed there were 6 New scratch off tickets on the kitchen table, I immediately called her daughter back and told her she had left some Scratch off tickets on the kitchen table, she told me, that those were mine, she had bought them for me as a gift also, I said oh my gosh! You have given me so much this Christmas, thank you for the wine and I had a lovely time at your house, Once I helped get her mom dressed for bed that night, I went into my room and began to thank god for another christmas day, another new year, even though wasn't with my family and missed being at home, I still had a good christmas at work, on Dec 29 I awoke and looked out my bedroom window and there was snow on the ground again, I went to take my shower and looked in Mrs. Nancy room and she was already up and sitting in the living room in her recliner, first thing she said to me was we got snow! I said yes and it's so beautiful, as time went on we got along very well, today saturday Jan 9, 2016 marks 65 year! Anniversary for Mrs. Nancy, it's a rainy day here in Massachusetts, but her daughter is still going grocery shopping, and afterwards she's taking her mother to visit her husband at the cemetery, so she can put his favorite chocolate Kitkat on her husband headstone, also a donut hole, and an anniversary card stating how much she miss and love him, when we returned the following saturday to the cemetery, the

Kitkat was still there but the donut hole was gone, and the card was still there, I told her daughter I thought the late night critters would have eaten it buy now, she replied yeah! I thought so too, we left the cemetery and she drove me and her mother back to her mother's place, later that day I prepared our lunch we had a roast beef sandwich and a salad, for our dinner we had lasagna, we watched a movie and around 10;30 pm I helped her get dressed for bed, today is Monday February 8, another snow storm here in Massachusetts, the city has closed all schools, and ask that if you have to drive please drop speeds to 30 miles per hour, its 18 degree weather, and the wind is 65 mph, all state & county business are closed due to power outages, today is February 14, 10;00 I'm getting my client up and dressed, then I'll prepare our breakfast, she likes to have oatmeal one slice of bacon, and a half piece of toast, she has had her breakfast, and took her morning Medicine and now, I will clean up the kitchen and assist her walking back to her favorite Recliner, where she slept from 10;30 until 2;00 pm, as i tried to wake her it was very hard, her daughter called me at 1;00 and i told her, her mother was still sleeping, she asked me how long had she been sleep I said about 3 hours now, she said she'd call back in another hour, when she did call back it was 2;00pm and Mrs. Nancy was still sleeping and would not answer to my call, her daughter stated that she was on the way over, and she will wake her up once she got there also she's bringing a three layer cake that her mother wanted for her birthday, once the daughter arrived she was able to wake her mom up, and let her know she had brought

her the cake she had requested, today is Feb 16, and Mrs. Nancy has turned 89, she has had her cake and ice cream with me and her daughter, it's been snowing now from 9;45 am until 4;00pm today is March 9, and I've been working here with Mrs. Nancy for 6 months now, this is a day after my birthday, yes I'm another year older but less in dept, Mrs. Nancy condition has began to get worse, one morning as I was preparing our breakfast, her daughter call every morning at 7 or 730 am, just to check on us, when the phone rang, I gave it to Mrs. Nancy, and she began to tell her daughter that I was holding her hostage, at that moment I knew that her Dementia was getting the best of her, her daughter asked her mom why did she think that, she could not give her daughter an answer, then she asked her mom to give me the phone, her daughter began to asked me what did I think was going wrong, I told her that her mother just woke up this morning more confused, and thinking that I was a stranger in her apartment!, even though I been here for 6 months, I told her daughter that I helped her get dressed for bed last night, we watched a movie, and had a little popcorn together, and when she woke up this morning, I went to help her get dressed She did not know who I was! And didn't want me to help her get dressed, or help her put on her support knee highs, which is always something she would ask me to do, because it's difficult for her to pull them on, in the last couple of months that I've been here, I had always helped her get dressed, so her daughter said that if she keep being confused, to give her a call back, and she would come and take her mother to the hospital .,so I left her

alone for awhile, so that she could dress herself, and I went to finish preparing our coffee and breakfast, when she was finished getting dressed, she came into the kitchen, I helped her to her seat, which was at the end of the table and placed her bib on her neck, as we were having our breakfast, the daughter called again at 7;30 as usual, her mother got up from the table before I could assist her, she walked into the living room to the phone without her walker,! I told the daughter, she didn't want my assistance with anything this morning, I told the daughter she got up so fast, she didn't even use her walker, they talked a while on the phone, in about 10 min the mother handed me the phone back, her daughter said that her mother was mumbling and she couldn't understand anything she was saying, I said to her, yeah I know that's how the dementia works, she said I'm glad you're there because I can't handle her mood swings, me and her daughter hung up from our conversation, after Mrs. Nancy was finished eating I began to clean up the kitchen, and gave her Mother her morning medicine for that morning, we watched a program on the TV, then we decided to go out for our afternoon walk outside, after the first walk outside, we came back inside the building, as we proceeded to go down the hall, she started knocking on the neighbors doors, telling them to call the police, call the police, because I was holding her hostage, I tried to tell her I live with you ', I'm here to help you, she told me I was a stranger, and she wanted me out of her building!!!, well One of her female neighbor, a friend of hers, she was about 85 years of age, she came out and tried to tell Mrs. Nancy, I had been there

caring for her over two months, and that I was not a stranger, I'm Only there to help her, well we could not calm her down, so I decided to call her daughter back, once I called the daughter on the phone, she could hear her mother in the background yelling and screaming at me, and her neighbor trying to calm her down, while her daughter talk to me on the phone, she could not talk any sense into her mom, she said to me just keep her Mother in the hallway, she was on the way to come and take her mother to the hospital, we did not go back into her apartment, we just sat in the lobby up front until her daughter pulled up, when she arrived, I helped her mother in the front seat of the SUV, and I proceeded to get into the back seat, once we arrived at Melrose Wakefield Hospital Emergency, she was still confused, and talking about things, myself, and her daughter did not understand,, they checked her in and the pre op nurse took her vital signs, and put her in a small room later a nurse came to tell us that they decided to keep her in the hospital, they also took urine sample, and said they will run more test on her overnight, the daughter drove me back to the apartment, well that overnight stay in the hospital, turned into week, then a month! Mrs. Nancy was about 5"4in and weighed only 100 pounds, while in the hospital, her daughter called me and said that her mother had lost 20 pounds, she wasn't eating, wasn't getting any better, I called my company to inform them Mrs. Nancy condition had gotten worse, and she was still in the Hospital, they came the following day, and picked me up from Mrs.Nancy apartment, which was located in Stoneham Massachusetts, and

took me to our office in Connecticut, which was a 2 hour drive, I stayed at the office apartment overnight, the next Morning I caught the Amtrak train and went home to Atlanta, for my two weeks vacation, when I returned back to work in Stratford Connecticut, which was a 17 hour ride back on the Amtrak train, my legs and body were exhausted, I arrived at the office and slept at the office apartment, until the next morning, or until the driver took me back to Mrs. Nancy, or updated me on her condition, I was told by One of our Nurses at Family Care, that she had passed, me and Mrs. Nancy daughter still keep in touch with each other, especially during football season, she is a Patriot fan, and I'm a Atlanta Falcon Fan, so we're always texting each other during the games, The company sent me to another case in Lynnfield Mass, they were preparing to get all the information on the Client, it was located at 4 Wildwood Dr, care for Mrs. Maria Rosatone, about 2;00 pm the driver took me to Mrs. Maria home, once we pulled up to her door, we could hear dogs barking, I began getting worried, because I did not want to work around large dogs, the small ones are okay, not more that 40 0r 50 pounds, and when she opened the door what did I see standing besides her, two huge dogs, one was jet black, and the other was solid white, each one looked to weigh over 120 lbs, me and the driver asked her ma'am please don't open the door, because I'm afraid of big dogs, she said don't worry, my son lives downstairs, and the dogs belong to him they live downstairs with him, she called her son to come and get his dogs, and close off the stairwell, so the dogs can't come up the stairs to the living room

where we are, the driver left and she began to show me to my room, once I began working with her, she told me she was 91, born on April 24, 1925, today February 21, 2016, she's still here to tell me the story, Maria is about 195 pounds, white med length hair, curled to the front of her face, and she still can do a lot for herself, she just repeats herself constantly, also hard of hearing, and ask have she eaten?, even if it's only been 15 min of her meal time, she still will ask you have she eaten yet? but she is a beautiful women especially when she puts on her makeup, at age 91 she don't look a day over over 60, when they lived in Italy, Maria told me that her Mother's, Mother lived to be a 100 years old, she also told me that her great grandmother was a Small frame beautiful woman, with solid white hair, and sky blue eyes, her grandmother suddenly died in the bed with her in Italy, when she was a little girl, Maria had two brothers, and two sisters, one of her brothers, died at age 17, of yellow fever, her older brother had came home for Easter, he was studying to be a doctor, and he died of pneumonia at age 19, She told me that her Mother went crazy, after losing both sons within a year, she said at night she would be sleeping in the bed with her mother, and never noticed that her mother was getting out bed going to the cemetery at night with a shovel, digging up her brother's grave, and saying come back to me, come back to me, until one night the Italian police officers came bangging on the door late one night, when she opened the door, the police had her mother in their Arms, they asked her did she know that every night your mother was going out to the cemetery, with a shovel trying to

dig up her sons ? yelling come back to me,  come back to me,  Of course she was hysterical, and said No No, Sir,  I had no idea my mother was getting out of bed and leaving me at night, the officer said that if she didn't stop they were going to lock her Mother up, so her Mother decided to move, and come to America, because the pain of losing both sons kept her depressed and the pain of grief was unbearable, so she decided to come with her mother, she was only 20 years old when they came over here to America she had one sister,  which was older than her, but her sister decided to stay in Italy, the older sister,  one of her sons was killed by a gang,  that was robbing people over in Italy,  and the police was trying to stop them, that gang killed 7 police officers that day, she began to tell me her sister was never the same after that, she lost her mind and died a couple years later, because she never got over her son being shot to death, Maria never got a chance to go back to visit her Sister in Italy,  The other sister had three kids, she died young in Italy in her early 30s of a stroke, Maria is hard of hearing and early stages of dementia, and I later learned,  as I began to live with Maria in her Home,  as we began talking each day,  one morning as I was preparing her breakfast, she stated to me she was Italian and loved to eat, for breakfast she would have toast orange juice grits bacon and a boil egg, as we sat at the table to have our breakfast, she began to tell me that she had been hit by a car, while walking her son two big dogs,  the same two dogs that are much bigger today! She would walk them near peabody Ma, every afternoon, and yes they meet me at her front door when I first arrived at her home, I

was so afraid Because they are taller than me when standing!, she stated that when she was hit by the car it split her stomach open, and she stayed in the hospital for months after the surgery, and from there she went to rehab for recovery, and she had to learn how to walk all over again,  before she returned home, a couple of weeks later, she fell outside on her stone pouch, and broke her hip, Oh my GOSH I said you have really been through it ! and as a result, she had to have hip replacement surgery, She told me she came to America in 1945, from a town called Calabria, in Italy,  City of Reggio Calabria, with her mom when she was in her early twenties, she told me she used to walk from her street across the track, all the way to peabody Ma,  and now she can barely get around, I told her she is still doing great to be 91, and able to tell me parts of her life history, and able to tell me how to cook real Italian food, at 91 Marie dresses very nice, and can still take her on shower, without assistant, but I sit at the door anyway and offer my help, she told me that she didn't want me to see here prsudore, which is what they called a lady private part in Italy,  I have learned a lot from working with Maria,  she is truly a unique women, when I left for my break to go home in Atlanta, after 10 weeks of working,  I visited one of my cousins church, and got a chance to go to my church also, which is something i can't do while traveling and working these cases, but I love what I do,  because the clients appreciate me, and I learn a lot from working with them, My church members were glad to see me, and i was glad to see them also, once I came back from Atlanta,  on March 22, of 2016,  which was my

last day with Maria, they sent another Nurse Aide to be with Maria Rosatone, because the first lady they sent there to relieve me, Maria didn't understand her language, so they sent another HHA to Maria, and they needed me on this new case in Auburn Mass, Once I arrived I noticed the house looked small, on the outside, with no garage, only a long driveway, but once i got inside and meet Mrs. Dorothy, she explained that this is a 3 floor home and she just stays on the middle floor, because she can't hardly get around to much and that's where the kitchen and the main bathroom is, and it's easy for her to get around the house, also there's another entrance and exit to the house, just in case of an emergency, she stated that she can't stand for long periods of time, because of her leg condition, later after working with her I learned that a quarter size sore was on her left leg, near her calf, and she often said that it hurted, and gave her problems, Ms. Dorothy Butkus, which is 86, and has a real bad skin Condition, weighs about 220 pounds, she's hard of hearing and wears oxygen to help with her breathing, and walks very slowly, even with a walker, so working with her, I had to speak louder, prepare her meals and she loves nothing but oatmeal in the mornings with lots of cinnamon, and a glass of orange juice, I'd get out her clothes to wear daily, drive to the grocery store or where ever she needed me to drive her, but she never wanted to go with me, but once just to show me around her neighborhood, because she complain that it was difficult for her to get in and out of her vehicle, because of her legs condition, so i learned the area pretty well, as i had to go shopping for us each week, she loved

Mcdonalds chocolate shakes, and every other day, she would send me to Mcdonalds, to get her and myself a chocolate shake, and she would add some TGI Fridays Mudslide, Mrs. Dorothy is a very sweet lady walks very slow, and she just seems to be a lonely woman that needs someone to talk to, so she enjoys company whenever possible, and we love to talk she said she never had a daughter, just one son, we talk a lot everyday about everything, I told her we had that in common, because i love to talk to, also i had only one son just like her, well today is Easter Sunday 3/27/16, me and Mrs.Butkus has had our Morning orange juice and Oatmeal, now we're waiting for her Beautician to bring her little dog toto back home, while she was away at St Vincent's Hospital, her friend the beautician has a Ranch, and kept her little dog toto, today will be there first day back together, so she's very excited her and the dog toto will be bonding again with each other, she was in the hospital for a month, well today is April 3, and I can't believe its Snowing here in Auburn Mass I've been here 12 days with Mrs. Butkus and toto, which is a very playful little brown Miniature shawawwar dog, April 4 Her Only Son came up from Austell Ga, where he and his family live, he came up to take his mother to One of her Appointments, that was concerning surgery on her leg, he stayed 4 days at a hotel, but came by each day to check on us, and took her to the hairdresser, they wanted me to go also, so that I could learn where it was, so I road with them to see where it was located, because once he leaves they both stated that I'll be the one to take her to and from the hairdresser, and anywhere else she

needed to go, I replied of course I will they often talked about her Moving to Ga, he stated to his mother, that he could not keep traveling back and forth to see about her, and keep taking her to all her Doctors appointments, so she should think about moving into an Assisted Living, or a Nursing Home, where she could be close to him, his wife and her two Grand boys, he told his mom the plans were to sell the house, and she move to Ga, but she did not like that idea! and stated to him that she did not want to move to Ga, because all of her friends was here in Auburn Mass, and she knew no one in Ga, and in a Assisted living you have to manage on your own, and she can't stand long enough to care for herself, that's why she hired me,!! I heard them Arguing each time he came over, about how she needed to move out of that house, and move to Ga, her son told her she was a selfish asshole, and she told him he was a spoiled ass hole, he told her he's the reason that I'm there helping her, and driving her to Grocery Store each week, because he knows that she can't drive or do shopping anymore, after he left that day, she told me that she and her late husband, had been in this house for over 45 years, his Mother & Sister also lived there, and some of their things were still in this house, and she doesn't want to leave it, and she doesn't think her son will treat her or her property with respect, if she moves near him in Ga, the next day when he came over I'm in the kitchen preparing dinner, I heard them Arguing again, over her Assets, after he left, she asked me what did I think, and I told her I can't get into their personal business, I'm only here to care for her, help her be Comfortable as possible, and do what

she needs to be done, around the house, I'm not getting into their business, well Thursday 3/31/16 he left, going back to Ga, after he had taken her to all of her doctors appointments, he told me thanks for caring for his mom, and she has all the help she needs, with me being there, the next day which was friday she told me her ribs were hurting, because of the way he lifted her into her car, after coming from her Appointments, she complained of that for at least 3 days, two days later when her lady friend of 25 years, came over to help her with paying her bills, and balancing her checkbook, she mention to her friend that she believe her ribs were broken or bruised, because they still hurt so bad, from the way her son had lifted her under her arms, and squeed around her chest, the following Wednesday 4/6/16 when her Visiting Nurse came to see her, she told the Nurse also, the Nurse told her that if it's bruised ribs, they will heal on their own, the next day after I prepared Mrs. Butkus breakfast, toto her dog would jump into her lap, eat all the crumbs, or whatever she had dropped in her lap, then he would put his head under her Blanket that was on her Lap, he did that after every Meal she had, and would stay there until she, put some food on a plate for him, or if she had to get up and go to the Restroom, at night that's where toto sleeps, in her lap under her blanket, she rarely laid in her bed, because of all the clutter of boxes of jewelry and clothes, some of which she kept on her queen size bed, I thought that was the reason she didn't sleep in her Bed, but she told me, that it was hard for her to get in and out when she has to use the restroom, so she just slept in her Large Brown

Recliner in the den, between the kitchen, and bathroom, toto her dog eats just about everything she eats, except for her chocolate cookies and shake, he even eats popcorn, that was my first time ever seeing a dog eat popcorn,! One day as me and Ms. Dorothy was putting away some of the clothes off of her bed, and she was clearing all the jewelry from off the bed and dresser, she gave me a 14 karat gold angel pendant, and told me I was an Angel, to do the work that I do, and later as we began to know each other, she would give me a piece of jewelry, every other day, until I had too much to carry with me, I had to ship some of it home to Atlanta, she said she used to just buy jewelry when she felt depressed and lonely, shoping always made her feel better, she told me she would buy it on sale, or if it was something she liked, she would buy it, some of this stuff she had was still in the packages never been open, but once I opened it, it was dry rotted and falling apart, she said some of it was her husband mother and she didn't want it, I didn't want it either so I looked in her phone book and found a goodwill called Big brothers & sisters, that would come and pick up old clothes and toys, and small furniture, there were a mink coat hanging in her room, and she said that it was supposed to be for her grandson, which is in college, but he never comes to visit her anymore, it was a Raccoon Coat, she ask me did I want them, which I was naive, because I never knew anyone made a Raccoon Coat, and I don't think I would want it, but after I saw it, I changed my mind quickly, after she told me I could have it, I told her it need to be washed, and there was a leopard wool coat hanging, she said

for me to try it on,  once I took the coat down off the hanger, and began to look at it,  before trying it on, I noticed there was mold inside of the sleeves, I showed it to Mrs. Dorothy,  she said that it could be washed, which she had a washer and dryer downstairs, so I washed all the coats she had given me including the Raccoon Coat, when I open the washing machine, I jump back! Because I thought a critter or something was in there, the Raccoon coat was in shreds !, Mrs. Dorothy said you were not supposed to wash that type of fur!!, well I had washed all the other coats, and they came out fine, I even dried the leopard coat in the dryer, I said I'm sorry!, I didn't know that it could not be washed, she said well don't worry, just put it in the trash, it's been here over 12 years and my Grandson never came to get it anyway, she asked me to take the other leopard coat, and the mink coat, she had given me so much jewelry, and makeup that had never been opened,  OMG so nice of her ! so I mailed some it home and told my daughter law she could have all that makeup,  once the package had arrived home in Atlanta, my daughter in law said when she opened the makeup it just crumbled up, I said yeah my client gave me all that make and jewelry, she said she has had it for years, and never opened,  I said she has a lot more and were just going to give it all to goodwill, and trash some of it,  well I had 8 bags of clothes to go to goodwill, the next day she had me to go upstairs and I had 8 more bags to fill full of old clothes and new shoes, that was left there by her husband dead mother and his deceased sisters, My whole day was just helping her get rid of some of her clothes and things she could not take to Ga, if she

decided to move there, I really liked staying there with MS DOROTHY, I feel the reason she shopped so much because she was bored, staying all alone in this 3three story house for over 30 years with nowhere to go, and nothing to do, I can understand why she enjoyed company and called me her angel, well my last day at Mrs. Dorothy house was June, 16 she told me she had decided to go ahead and move to Ga in an Assisted living near her ass hole son, well when I left Mrs. Dorothy, I forgot to get the coats, I was sent another suitcase after I came back from Atlanta on my two week break from Ms. Dorothy, My company sent me to another case that was located in North Adams, because the lady they have there now, has no control over the client, the client is running all over her, and she has no control of the situation, and they need someone that's firm but nice, that can take charge, so I took on the case, as the Driver was taking me there its way up near the Mountains, all you could see were hills, the Appalachian Trail, the Hoosac trail, . . . North Adams Massachusetts was a 2 hour and 35 min drive from our office in Stratford, as we were driving up there it seemed like 4 hours, instead of two and a half, all you could see were trees, and large Tree hills, and mountains, once i arrived it was a beautiful home, I could look out the kitchen window and her side door, see the top of the hills nothing but green tall hills as far as you can look!, early in the morning you can see fog coming off of the hills, it looks like smoke coming from a huge volcano, It's a beautiful place to see, early in the mornings, her house was all wood interior with three levels, I'm told it's made of yellow pine,

heavy enough to keep the bears out, its built very sturdy, some people around in her neighborhood, told her that bears lived up in the big green hills, Mrs. Donna Danis, was born July 19,1942, while working for Mrs. Donna I learned that her husband of 45 years, had been a North Adams police offer for 40 years, he had been deceased for about 12 years now, he also had been in the Army for two years, they had two sons, which one is retired from the army, and one has been in the army for 21 years, on July 25, of 2016, as we were sitting at her dining room table, she began to tell me her husband collected small sport cars and Hess 18 wheeler trucks,, she said he told her since he couldn't afford to buy the real ones, but he could buy the small ones, she took me to her basement downstairs, where she also kept an extra refrigerator, and began to show me all these toy cars that had never been open, three of her walls were full, from the floor up, about 6 feet tall,! boxes and boxes of new all kinds of Hot Wheel cars !! Miniature jaguars, miniature Lamborghini, so many die cast cars, and trucks, it would take three whole days or more to count them all, All I could say was wow, WOW!! my grandson would have a ball in here !, She said her Son had a tag sell one day, and a lady was outside her house at 6;00 am waiting to get one of those miniature cars, or one of those Hot wheels, she said her Nephew sold one of those cars online for 65$dollars!, one little tiny car, well we finally left the basement, and went back upstairs, she asked me to get out this big bag from under the bed where her husband used to sleep, after he had gotten sick, I began to pull out this huge white bag, that had lots of

cards and envelopes inside, they looked like holiday cards, or Birthday cards, I pulled out one large envelope, that contained, two cards, of which she told me, that one was a Birthday Card from her husband, she asked me to read it : With loving thoughts, to my wife, The Anniversary Card, read: With Love to my wife on our Anniversary, inside it read; You are the most important person in my life, I love you, I need you, and I treasure you always, Happy Anniversary, but they were not signed by her husband,, she told me that she found the cards a couple of months, after he died, he told her before he died that he bought her some cards, but couldn't remember where he had put them, so now on every Anniversary, and Birthday, she has a card from her loving husband of 45 years, even though he didn't live long enough to sign or give them to her, she still treasures those two cards, and has them to look at, it's been 10 years today since her husband passed, on Aug 22,16 Mrs. Donna had slipped on her stairwell, trying to go down stairs, to put food in her refrigerator, located in the basement, I immediately called her son Shun and told him she had slipped on the stairs, which we had told her to stay off the stairs, unless she was with me, well after she slipped she walked back upstairs, and began to help me prepare our dinner, we had our dinner, and later that night we had Coffee Ice Cream, which was her favorite, and later I began to help her get dressed for bed, she began to tell me that her side and back was aching, I called her son again, and informed him that she was now complaining of back and side Pain, he said to call her friend Babara of 60 years that knew all her Medical history, she

would know what to do, But Ms. Donna did not want me to call Mrs. Barbara, because she said, Mrs. Barbara would talk her to death, and she didn't feel like talking, so I checked over her upper body, to make sure that she didn't have any bruises from the slip on the stairs, and gave her a tramadol for pain, well there were no bruises, I still asked her did she want me to call 911, she stated NO! just give me the pain pill, and I will be ok, only a carpet burn was on her elbow, which I noticed, and I cleaned it with peroxide, and called her son anyway to let him know, the next day he brought me a note to give to her doctors, the NOTE read Please add Melinda to the list of people who can talk to the Doctor, and then he left, and said he had an appointment to go to, well around 12:30 am that night, Mrs. Donna called me back into her Bedroom, and said that it hurt for her to move, and when she breath it hurts, I thought to myself, she has damaged her ribs, I knew from my experience working in the Hospital, that's what it sounded like to me, so I called her friend Mrs. Barbara, and told her what happen, because she knew all of her medical history, and had been with her through 2 strokes, and a fall which happen 5 years back, when she was staying alone in this house, she had fell downstairs off of a milk crate, trying to put up shower curtains in the downstairs shower, and hit her head, so when Mrs. Barbara arrived she looked at her and asked her could she get into her car ?Mrs. Donna stated no, because it hurt her to move, also Mrs. Donna has osteoporosis, Hypertension, and anxiety disorder, so she has to be very careful of falls and injuring herself, well after she told Mrs. Barbara that

she could not get into her car, she told me to call 911, because Mrs. Donna said that she could not move, or get off the bed, so I immediately called 911 and about 10 min, 4 firemen and 2 paramedics arrived, I let them into the house and escorted them to her bedroom they put her on a flat hard plastic board, wrapped her up with a sheet, and put her in the ambulance, Myself and Mrs. Barbara proceeded to follow the ambulance in her car, to BMC emergency room, which was Berkshire Medical Center, once we got there, and they checked her over which it was about 2;30 am when they finished with Mrs. Donna, and the Nurse came out to tell us what was wrong, the Nurse stated that Mrs. Donna had 6 fracture ribs, on her left side, right above her old fracture! And her lower back vertebrae was fractured also, they had to put her on a brace to keep her from bending, or twisting, because if she twisted the wrong way she could paralyze herself, so she stayed in the hospital for two days, on the second day, the hospital called and said that she would be released, and that we could come and pick her up, I called Mrs. Barbara to let her know, she stated that they had called her also, and that she would come pick me up, and we would go to BMC, to get Mrs. Donna, when we got there, and walked into Mrs. Donna room she was sitting in her chair, with a black brace on, after about an hour, the doctor and Nurse came in to give us the Discharge papers, and said she would have to wear the TLSO Brace when out of bed, and walking around, when we arrived home Mrs. Donna used the restroom, and I prepared her for bed, after a small snack, she has been wearing her brace as instructed, for a week

now, and I'm told she will have it for about 4 more weeks, I had planned to take my vacation on September 20-Oct 10 but her family has said that they didn't want anyone else to care for Mrs. Donna, also when a caregiver leaves, they say that they will come back to care for her, but they never come back! I told her son that I always come back to my Clients, it's the Company that sends us on other cases, and puts another caregiver in my place while I'm away, well he and his wife said that they did not want another caregiver, because she has had 5 different ones, and they never came back, so I said Okay I'll stay with her until she gets better, And maybe by November first, I can take my two or three weeks off, just tell the company that you request for me to come back here,, after my vacation, I will gladly come back because your Mother is a sweetheart, just a little stubborn sometimes, and she loves her coffee Ice Cream !!they all agreed that yes she is Stubborn, because she was spoiled by their Dad, and she has always been an independent women, living all alone in this house, and doing for herself since her husband died 10 years ago, I'm still here with Mrs. Donna, and she is doing well, still wearing the brace while out of bed walking around the house, and she doesn't go near the down stairs anymore, I will go down the stairs to wash our clothes, and to put extra food in the refrigerator downstairs, she also has physical therapy that comes three times a week, to help strengthen her lower body, she and I do the exercises together, during the day and she likes that, it gives us both something extra to do, well it's 9;00 am, time for me to go and wake Mrs. Donna, and help her get

dressed, give her morning Medicine prepare our breakfast, and get our Day Started! Well it's time for me to take my two week break, I've been here with Mrs. Donna for three Months now, I'll be taking a vacation from Sept 28-Oct 17, going home to Atlanta enjoying my little One bedroom Apartment, located in the heart of Greenbriar, today is Oct 19, I've arrived back in Connecticut, and our company driver will take me to North Adams Massachusetts back to Mrs. Donna home, I arrived at Mrs. Donna home late that evening, I exchanged information with the caregiver that was there, she informed me Ms. Donna already had her supper, so her and the driver left going back to Connecticut to the office, which was a 2 hour drive, I was glad to be back with Ms. Donna, and she said she was glad to have me back also, so we chatted a little bit, then I helped her get ready for bed, on the next Morning together we fixed our Morning Breakfast, she began to tell me, that her and her son went to look at an assisted living for her, as me and Mrs. Donna was having our lunch in Tv room that evening, her son Shun and his wife came by to visit, as I was looking at the tv, the wife motioned for me to turn down the volume on the TV, she began to tell me that they had found a place for Mrs. Donna, it was a lovely place, and they think she will love it, next Sunday Oct 30,16 she will be moving into the Assisted living called Sugar Hill, located in Dalton Massachusetts, and that will be my last day with her, but they ask me could I stay until that Monday, Oct 31, I agreed to stay until that Monday me and Mrs. Donna went to the Oriental Buffet, across street from her home, where we had gone many times

before and had our last lunch together, we laughed and said how much we will miss each other, my company driver picked me up later on that Monday Evening and took me back to our Office in Stratford Connecticut, they have a new case for me, today Nov 2, I'm going with an open mind and caring heart, because you never know the situation until you get there, I arrived at Mrs. Rosemode Robinson home she's 91,born Nov 1 1925, same as my oldest sibling Franklin birthday NOV 1, Mrs. Robinson lives alone at 34 Cape Cod, in Redding Massachusetts she's a retired high school Math teacher, her husband was a teacher also at the same school, he used to teach Math for the 7th graders, but he had a Major in Social Studies, she told me he passed in early June of a bad heart, he also tutored students during the summer, they had been married for 40 years, he told her that a couple of the students, were walking down the hall, and said to him Nice buns Mr.D, as he was walking into his class, so when he got home he ask her well what do you think, and turned his butt to her, Mrs. Robinson said to him what do they know, they are only a bunch of laughing 13 year olds, she stated that her husband was a popular junior high teacher, in 1977 she taught french to third graders, and after that she taught french and spanish to seniors, in Hanover New Hampshire, before she got married to her husband, who was teaching at Wakefield, she was teaching at Stoneham Mass, they meet at a club where all the college graduates use to go, they got together and brought their first house in 1958 in Redding Mass, they both continued to date, and travel to different parts of town to teach, until they had

furnished the house, her husband was the first to move into the home, she moved in a little later, they bought twin beds, a sofa and a Kitchen set, and two chairs, which she still has today ! way over 50 years old, she told me the sofa and One chair has been upholstered once, in 58 years, today Nov 7 2016, Myself and Mrs. Robinson had our first outings, she took me to this place called red heat tavern, Oh my gosh you will not believe how nice and beautiful the seating was, the look of leather with diamond studs around the edges of the booth seat, I'm sure they weren't REAL Diamonds, but they sure looked like it! the tables were made of solid oak wood covered with glass!, well after i finished admiring the scenery,, we were seated by one the waiters, they gave us a booth, window side, which I loved, we sat down and begin to look at the menu, she began to tell me they had the best fresh seafood in Woburn Mass, and they will cook it as ordered, of course I ordered the seafood platter, and she order the shrimp and clams dinner, when they brought the platters they were full to the top fresh fish galore, two people could get full off of one plate! as we began to eat, they brought over beverages, in these lovely wine glasses, I asked Mrs. Robinson, I wonder will they sell me One of these glasses,? I would love to have one as a souvenir, She replied YES I'm sure they will, just ask the waiter when she comes back to our table, and I did, and yes said the waiter, I'll bring you One back, when the waiter brought one wine glass back, Mrs. Robinson said why don't you get two, I was thinking the same thing, deja vu !!then I asked the waiter could she Please bring another wine glass? they had the Words

RED HEAT written in RED, we finished our dinner, and went back to the house, Me and Mrs. Robinson took off our shoes, put on our night clothes, and meet back downstairs, she didn't have a TV, so we talked a lot, well she talked about her life and I listen, she began to tell me she attended Catholic school, from 1st grade to College, and she had the same order of NUNs from 1st-8th grade, Sister of the assumption Nuns,9 thru college was a bonding school, located in Hudson New Hampshire, the name of the school was Presentation of Mary, she began to tell me that the NUN Teachers were very strict, the students could not talk, or laugh out loud in class unless given permission, One day one of their Priest name Father D came by to visit, and he noticed that some of the girls in her class, were heavy chested, and stated to the teacher that something had to be done, so the Nun cut out a long square piece of unbleached cotton, the teacher Nun asked the heavy chested student to come up front, and she asked two other girls to stand by on each side and wrap the cloth around the girl chest, and pull tight, while the Nun used a safety pin to secure it in the back, she said it was so uncomfortable, the NUNs called it a special made bra, but the girls complain about it among themselves, there were 15 girls in her class, one of the girls parents, lived near buy, so they would pick her up at 12;00 for lunch and bring her back to the school by 4;00 pm, because the girls were not allowed to stay out overnight, they can stay out only a few hours during day, with their Parents to out to Dinner, with family or a movie, as she was out with her parents, her mother noticed she seemed very pale, and

asked her daughter what was wrong, so after they arrived home, she began to tell her mother that the Nuns made them special bras! For the heavy chested girls, all though she wasn't as heavy chested as some of Girls, the Nun still made her one, so her mother asked to see the special Bra, when her Mother saw this long unbleached cotton cloth, tight around her daughters chest! She was so upset, but didn't say anything to the NUN about it, because that NUN was a Superio, the one in charge, and what she says goes, NO one could change it! So the student went back to all of her classes, after visiting with her parents, and she continue to go there for 4 years, she said once she Graduates, she won't ever come back, but once she Graduated, she still came by the school to visit, they had one NUN called the disciplinarian, she was very strict! It would be a 100 girls in study hall, and you could not hear a pencil or a pen fall! Well today is Nov 9, 16 me and Mrs. Robinson are going out to Dinner, at another Seafood Restaurant, called Lobster Claw, located on 3 Main St in North Reading MA, when we walked inside, their were two front glass doors, on each side, and the second thing I noticed was this HUGE RED Lobster hanging on the side of the wall, and in front of the doors was a man, made of a ship captain, holding the ship steering wheel, with a yellow long coat, and a yellow captain hat, very unique! i told Mrs. Robinson I had never seen anything like this before, she replied I know, because this is the only one in this part of Massachusetts, when we placed our orders, I had jumbo shrimp, and she ordered Haddock Fish & fries, when the plates arrived, I said WOW this is a lot of food, the waiter

replied we do that, to give our customers their money's worth, the plates were stacked to the top, after about 4 shrimps, I was full, with plenty to take back home, she could not finish her fish and fries either, she only ate two of her pieces of fish, and handful of the fries, and still had 3 pieces of fish and plenty of the fries to take back home, 36.25 was the total for both of our dinners, again a big surprise to me, I thought it would be much more than that, we enjoyed our dinner, now were are headed back home, and I help her get ready for bed, and I will go upstairs to my room and get myself ready for the next Morning, well today is another nice day her with Mrs. Robinson, when I came down stairs this morning, Mrs. Robinson asked me would I like to drive her to Wilmington Ma, I said sure, she said there was a tavern called RED Heat, and we will have lunch there, when we arrived we were seated by one of the waiters at a booth, she gave the both of us a menu, the meals started at 16.00 dollars, so I didn't want to order anything too expensive, but before I could ask her anything, Mrs. Robinson she said order whatever you like, I said okay I'll try the Salmon with baked asparagus, topped with chopped pistachios, she ordered the chicken with the sesak salad, when the food arrived to my surprise, the salmon was sitting on top of a bed of sweet mashed potato ! I told Mrs. Robinson I had never seen salmon prepared that way, the food looked mouth watering, and was very delicious! I must say up here in Massachusetts, you might pay a little more for eating out, but you will get you money worth !From Oriental to Seafood, it's all good and fresh, she stated the seafood is always plentiful,

because we are near Boston, where all the fresh seafood comes from, before we left I asked the waiter could I buy one of the wine glass that has the name RED HEAT on it, she said yes I'll bring you one back, Mrs. Robinson said to me why don't you buy two, I said well I will have to see how much room I have in my suitcase, I don't want to buy it, and it gets broken before I reach GA, so I'll just purchase one for now, she said okay, maybe will come back up here for lunch before you leave, today is Nov 12, 16 Mrs. Robinson and myself, went back to the RED HEAT Tavern, for lunch, and I purchased another wine glass, now I have a set, and of course I ordered the salmon over mashed sweet potatoes um um good, this time it was even better than before, Mrs. Robinson ordered a different kind of chicken, going out to a nice fancy restaurant like this, I will never order Chicken ! well we had our lunch, and I drove back home, we sat in the living room until about 8;30 pm talking, about her life as a child, and when she started dating her husband, and after she graduated from the school of Nuns, well now it's time to start preparing her bed now, afterwards and I will head upstairs to my room for the night, and see what tomorrow brings, well we made it thru the night, I'm gonna get myself dressed, and I'll go down stairs to help her get dressed, once dressed in the morning we sometimes have coffee or hot tea, and then she decides where she wants to go for lunch and dinner, Mrs. Robinson stated that she would like to go back to the Lobster Claw, because her niece called this Morning, and said that wednesday the 16, might be my last day with here, because she wants someone to come 2 hours in the

Mornings, and two hours at night, to help her, and my company do not have assignments for that type of help, but i said to her but there are other companies in MA, that might accommodate her schedule, so for lunch we went back to the Lobster Claw, I ordered the bay shrimp & strips for 15.95, Mrs. Robinson ordered the clam plate for 22.95, once they brought our food, it was a lot! And again we had plenty to take back home, after we finished eating and got back to her car, I noticed that the left driver side tire, was very low and needed some air, so I told Mrs. Robinson we should stop at a service station, so they could check out her tire, as I began driving up North Reading toward home, we stopped at 3 service station, and they all said they were closed, because it was on a Sunday! I thought if they saw a black woman, with a white old woman, maybe they would try to help us, not a chance, so we kelp driving alone and we finally found a Gas station wear I saw, a car was there getting serviced, so i immediately pulled in, and a white gentleman came and asked could he help us, we said yes please!, we've stopped at 3 stations and they all said they were closed, he replied don't worry I'll take care of it, she told him she needed some gas, so he put in the gas, and air into all of her tires, that needed it, when he was done she offered to pay him, and he said no problem you ladies have a nice day! And we both smiled at each other, and I said there's a silver lining always down the road, Yes Ma'am replied Mrs. Robinson, his heart was in the right place at the right time, so there are still some generous people in this town, after about 2 hours of riding around to fine air and gas, we finally arrived

back to her home safety, we had clam chowder soup for dinner, and I helped her get ready for bed, we didn't talk to much that night, I think because we were so full, so I went upstairs to my bathroom and had my shower and off to bed I went, the next morning I got up, got myself dressed, and headed down stairs, to help her get dressed, but when I reached the end of the stairwells, I could see her sitting in the living room, in her favorite chair, staring at the wall, I said good morning, or you okay,? you're up very early, she replied yes I know, I was just sitting here thinking of where we could go today for lunch, I was surprised because we had been going out to eat everyday, since last week, so I figured she would be tired of going out, because she knows that I can cook, and we have plenty of haddock chowder, which is one of her favorite dishes, Mrs. Robinson asked me have I ever been to a place called Joe Fish, in North Reading, I said no ma'am, as soon as she asked me the question about Joe Fish my phone rang, it was Adrian from the Office in Stratford Connecticut, saying that friday the 18 will probably be my last day with Mrs. Robinson, because her niece only wants someone in the mornings for 2 hours, and 2 hours at night to make sure she gets into bed, and up the next morning to take her Meds, after talking with them, Mrs. Robinson heard the conversation, and said well we may as well go up Joe fish and have our last lunch together, I drove us to joe fish, and we had our lunch, the seafood was delicious, today is friday the 18, and Mrs. Robinson has gotten more independent, and doing more for herself, so my company said her physical therapy will continue for next couple of

weeks, and they will monitor her and see how good she does on her own again, and also they will be getting her meals on wheels, since she can't drive anymore, and she won't have to do any cooking, well the driver picked me up on the 18 and took me to the office in Connecticut, I spent the night upstairs above the office for the weekend, Monday morning, Adrian the office assistant, came to tell me they had another case for me in Ridgefield Connecticut, at 640 Danbury Rd, Benchmark Assisted Living, where I would be assisting Mrs.Mary Ann, who has early stages of dementia, and her husband lives there also, and he's a hospice patient, when myself and the driver arrived at Benchmark Assisted living, we were greeted by a staff member that pointed us to the frontdesk, the lady behind the desk ask for our I.D., we showed it to her, then she asked us to sign in to their logbook, My driver told her that he was only dropping me off to care for one the Clients that lived there, then she said for me to sign in, after I signed the book, she began to call upstairs to the clients room, to let them know I was here, as the driver left, he ask was I ok, I said yes I'm just waiting for the Daughter of Mrs. Mary Ann to meet me here, as I turned away from the desk I saw a middle age women coming towards me, and of course it was the daughter, she introduced herself as Suzanna, we began to walk down the hall to the elevators, and she began to tell me some things about her mother and father, that they both are declining rapidly, her mother is 81, an born on Sep 20, 1935, she had six kids, 3 girls and 3 boys, but you would never know she had 6 kids, she weighs only 106 pounds and 4'9 feet tall, and she

dresses very well, as I began to live there and work with her, I learned from one of her daughters that she was a retired Deputy Mayor, and trustee, from 1996-2001, for the Village of Larchmont, located in West Chester County, in New York State, I've had the pleasure of meeting all of her kids, this is a two bedroom, very spacious apartment, this facility does everything for them, they have housekeeping everyday, that changes there towels and bed linen, also they serve 3 meals a day, and they can have their food brought up to their rooms, if they don't feel like going down to the dining room, and my meals are free, just feel out a meal slip of what I want, each morning for breakfast, and also in the afternoon when the menu comes out for dinner, just circle what I want on the menu for that day, and put it in the drop box near the kitchen downstairs, and they will prepare it and bring it up to the room the following morning, also I take her mother to the dining room for lunch and dinner, when she feels up to going, if she don't want to go they will deliver it to the room, Suzanna her daughter came by the next day and we began to talk, she begin to tell me within two weeks, her Mother condition began to decline and sometimes they don't understand what she is saying, not only does she speak soft but in low voice also, she said her Mother and father sleep in separate rooms, and the Caregiver they had before me, her mother decided that she didn't like her anymore, that's why they decided to get someone more experienced, and just another face for her to look at, I began to tell her that's how dementia works, One day they like you, the other days they may not know who you are, her mother

had gotten to the point where she would push her disabled husband out of bed, and he could not walk, so the nurses and housekeepers would have to come to there room late at night and pick him up off the floor, so that's why the family decided to put them in separate rooms, I explained to the daughter Mrs. Suzanne that I was experienced with Dementia,, and Alzheimer's disease, I've been in this field for 24 years, and all dementia patients react differently, and that disease slowly progress over time, so you have to have patience's with them, and just try to make them feel comfortable as possible with you, I told her I used to have a client that went through 8 H.H.A .caregivers, before she was satisfied, That's how dementia works, she replied I know, that's what I don't have is patience, because I have a husband and two kids at home and I'm trying to run and be at both places, and its hard, so thank you again for your help! And I'm glad we found someone experienced with this type of Dementia, She stated to me that her dad can not do anything for himself anymore and he's in hospice care, her mother and father had been Married for 58 years, I said Wow ! that's a long time, I know they love each other dearly, her dad has around the clock care from this facility and through Hospice Care, on Dec 23 16, I've been working here for 35 days, Mr. Richard took his last breath, surrounded by all of his kids, He had been ill for several years his son & daughters told me, But the mother has been ill for only about 7 months, I told Suzanne that in reality nothing is going to change how her mother feels about a person, we just have to deal with her daily as each situation arises,

her daughter just nodded her head in amazement and sadness, and said thank you again for taking care mom, because both parents were sick at the same time, Mrs. Mary Ann was a very petite Lady, small frame, short white hair cut into a bob style, and dressed business attire everyday, I asked her daughter what type of work did her Mother do before she got sick ?, she said her mother was a Deputy Mayor for years In her County,  I told her I can tell she was a professional by the way she carry herself, and the way she likes to dress, she told me they had a dog also that her mother and father loved dearly, so they hired a dog walker, to come and take the dog for walks twice a day, Morning and at night,  I continued staying there to care for Mrs. Mary,  I had to sleep on a sofa bed that was in the living room, which was located right between the both of them, or I could sleep in her mothers room with her, because there were two twin beds in the Mother room,  and Only one bed in the father room, so I decided to sleep on the sofa bed just to feel things out and get used to my surrounding,  also I could hear her in the middle of the night, after the daughter left, I began to sit on the sofa with the Mother Mrs. Mary Ann, and try to talk with her,  she sat there with a book in her hands, as if she was reading,  and ignored me all the time, so I just kept talking anyway, the dog jumped on the sofa right between her and myself, since she would not talk to me,  I started doing some crossword puzzles, and asked her would she like to do one with me,  she looked at me real hard, and took the paper out of my hands, and began to look at it, she stared at it for about 12 seconds,  then she passed it back to me,  and said ok your

turn, I took the paper back and began to find a word, before I could finish circling the word she ask for it back, and said something to me, and smiled, but I could not understand what she was saying, because she speaks with a low and soft voice, just as her daughters had told me, this dog is a pitbull, and he jumps all over the furniture, including the sofa bed where I sleep, and every morning there is dog hair all over my clothes, when I sit in the chairs by the window dog hair is all over it, and I don't know how to get rid of it, the dog sleeps on the bed with the mother, so dog hair is always on her bed covers, and all on her clothes, One morning when housekeeping came, I asked for a lint brush, and a lint sticky roller, after I took Mary Ann down for lunch, I put my order in for my lunch and went back to the room and tried to clean up some of that dog hair from the sitting areas, the next morning dog hair was back all over the place, so at that point I waited a couple of days, before I cleaned it up again, One morning before Mr. Richard had passed, the Nurse came in the room at 5;30 am and said she was there to get him up, because he's supposed to be up by 6.00 am, because she has about 5 more people to get bathe and dressed before breakfast, I was not happy with them just entering the room without even a knock or warning, they had keys so they would just come in at anytime, I'm sleeping right here in the open living room, so now they don't come in as often, just to give Mary her meds three times a day, so I'm kind of prepared for that, but I still have to be up by 5;00 am to get myself together, fold up the sofa bed, and just sit until my lady wakes up, then I will get her bathed and

dressed and see if she wants to go down for breakfast, or should I have them bring it up to the room for her, I know dealing with her type of Dementia it will be a different situation daily, but this is what I Do,, so I just try to prepare myself mentally, and remember to stay focused, she has a long separate eating table in the room, so before she start eating, if she ate in the room, I can sit her table as if she were in the dining room, every morning before the Aides and Nurses starts entering the room, I had to make sure everything was in place and out of there way, I've been here three weeks now, and this was getting to be so uncomfortable, with the Nurses coming in all time of night, and the dog hair all over my clothe, I'm not liking this set up at all, but her daughters & family shows me so much respect, and they appreciate my help and care for their mother, so I will deal with this living arrangement until the end, because this is why it's called long term care, sometimes it's better to just be still and move slowly, because our blessings could be right where we are, but we can't see it for the situation were in, but I stayed even though I was a little uncomfortable with the midsize pitbull dog staring at me all the time, maybe he wasn't used to seeing a different color, or something, I don't know why he likes staring at me, today is november 30, I received a call that Mrs. Mary brother was coming to visit her today, so after I picked her up from the dining room, from eating her lunch, we went back to the room, and she began to take off her shirt, I said Mrs. Mary it's not bedtime what are you doing? She didn't speak to me at all, she just kept trying to take off her blouse, and I was trying to keep it on her, I

said Mrs. Mary your brother is coming to see you in a little while,, I went back and forth with her almost 40 min, trying to keep her from taking off her clothes,, so I finally got her to keep her blouse on, and sit on the sofa, and at 1;40 her brother Bill arrived, when I opened the door, the dog ran and jumped all over him, as if he knew him, Bill sat on the sofa bed where I sleep at night, and he begin to talk with his sister, she crossed her leg and folded her arms, but didn't say much, so her brother asked me how was she doing? I told him she just finished going back and forth taking her clothes on and off, and I know she should be exhausted, but her brother said i don't think so, because in her situation, she will overwhelm you, before she gives up, and he was so right !,, Mrs. Mary began to tell me that he was the rich brother, I asked her why did she call him that, I looked at her brother bill and he just smiled, as Mary began to tell me that he owned his own Jet, and had asked her to be his guest at the White house, they arrived at the white house in one of his private planes, I said his plane WOW! That's real Cool, she said he has all three, a plane, a private jet, and a helicopter, I replied OKAY !now I see why she calls him the rich brother, his wife name is Hillary, same as Bill Clinton wife, I told him if he ever ran for President he would definitely have my vote, Bill told me that his only regrets are that he didn't take his education more seriously, and he thinks that everyone should try to do whatever there dream is in this life, he really gave me something to think about, on thanksgiving day her other son Hayes and his wife Katie and there two sons came to visit, I was looking

out her window as other residents, family and love ones came to pick them up for thanksgiving, cars would be lined up all around the building, I was sad that day wishing I was home cooking food for my family, on Dec 5 around 9;58 am after breakfast, Mrs. Mary had her first fall as we were leaving out of the bathroom, that's when I noticed she was getting very weak, I called her daughter Suzanne, which was the contact person, and informed her that her mother had just fell as we were coming out of the bathroom, she just fell back and her head hit the closet door, as I was on the phone with her, the nurse aide had just came in the room, to bring her medicine, Suzanne said to call the ambulance, I told her there were no bruising I could see, no visible cuts or blood, she said okay, she would meet us at the hospital and she would talk to me more once we get there, Me and the aide took Mrs. Mary vital signs so we could give them to EMS when they arrived, which was at 10;40 am, we arrived at the emergency room at 11;00 and they took Mrs. Mary to get a CT Scan, at 11;35 she was back from CAT, and at 12;35 her daughter Suzanne arrived at the hospital, also her other daughter Mary, and we were talking, they informed me to always call them if the doctors talk about keeping their mother in the hospital, because that's what they don't want, the doctor came into the room at 2;25, and stated that her cat scan was clear, and she was free to be discharged, her daughter Mary had brought her clothes but forgot to get her shoes, but with the three of us we managed to get her into the car, with only hospital shoes on her feet, which she did not like! Mrs. Mary has three beautiful

daughters, Jennifer the Nurse, everyone calls her the nurse of the family,  because she works at Northern Westchester Hospital, (Psychiatric Dept) her daughter Mary Ann is a school teacher, she's a Go and Get it done type of lady, and her daughter Suzanne is the Emotional One, she's very sensitive to certain situations, there the sister which I always wanted but never had,  they all played a very important part in their Parents life, which I had not seen in too many other families where I've worked before, they have shown nothing but love and compassion,  and they take took turns coming to see about their parents, whatever I needed or there mother, they just bought it and more, they never hesitated, they just worked together and got it done, also they are very understanding of my job here especially when they knew their mother was a handful, I stayed calm and kept my composure, I can say that this is a caring family,  even though their mother health is steadily declining,  they made sure there parents had the very best of Home Care, and they wasn't the self-righteous type, that I've seen in other families,  they all took time out of their busy lives to visit there mother every day, I started this case on Nov 18,  16 well this case has lasted 56 days, but it seemed much longer ending on Jan 13,17,  it has been an amusing and very interesting, and at times overwhelming case, But I enjoyed every minute of it. They decided to put their mother into around the clock more skilled nursing care, which is located just in the next building, because of her declining health,  so I'm moving on to my next case,  Once I come back from Atlanta on my three week break, well I'm back from Atlanta, visiting friends and my

family, today is Feb 13, 17 and the company has informed me that my New case is located at, 287 lambert Cove Rd, in Vineyard Haven Massachusetts, which is inside of Martha's Vineyard, and the only way to get there is by ship or plane ! I have never been on a ship before so this should be very interesting, the following day the driver took me and my suitcase to the shipyard, where I had to purchase a Martha's Vineyard ticket before I could get on the ship, but the company paid for it, although it was only 7;00 one way, when I saw that huge huge ship that had Martha's Vineyard on it I started snapping pictures, and all the water oh my god this was a sight to see, Once you get off the ship you are at a cab stand which will then take you to the clients home, the cab was 17;00 dollars, which I got reimbursed from the company, it was about a 15 min ride to there house, after I arrived at Mr. and Mrs. Mullins home, the first thing the wife showed me was the house that Princess Diana lived in when she wanted to getaway and just Relax, this a beautiful Island surrounded by beaches, lagoons, and white doves, I've finally seen a white sea dove in real life, when you walk out their back door you're on a beach! Wow this is a Beautiful home I was saying to myself water as far as your eyes can see, you can see other homes across the water, it looks to be about 10 miles across and 3 miles wide, I found lots of seashells, crabs, and oysters, all in her backyard that had washed up from the water ! as I kept waking, I saw a bridge that someone had built to get across, of course I took lots of pictures to send home, as we went back into her house she began to tell me about her husband, and his

condition, Mr. Mullins is 81 and has parkinson disease, he's 6,4 in height when standing, and weights about 205 pounds he is not bedridden, but he shakes a lot and needs lots of attention, that's why its two caregivers to care for him, me another lady from Jamaica, but she works for our company, the wife showed us our room which was down the hall from where her and her slept, there were two twin beds all made up very nice as a guest room, across the hall was our bathroom just for us to use and shower, there were new hand and face towels, also big bath towels a closet to store our personal items, body wash etc., the house was flat level no stairs at all, it was long ranch style with the kitchen and dining room in the middle, and of course a double glass patio door, leading out to the balcony and the beach, me and my other caregiver once we were in our room that night we decided to do everything together, when working with Mr. Mullins, because it was a lot to be done and his wife wanted it done precise and on time, so we worked together, when getting him up and getting him dressed, on Feb 20 we took Mr. Mullins to his dentist appointment, I saw the oldest bank called the Santander Bank it's made of all oblong off white stone, just beautiful I've never seen a bank made of all stone, it looked expensive and rich, then i thought to myself I am in Martha's Vineyard, they have all their own everything, on the same street, grocery store, drug store, library, kids clothing store, vitamin store, and a bookstore, also his wife took us into this restaurant after Mr. Mullins was finished with his dental appointment, it was small but sold large amounts of food, I ordered the salmon sandwich, and it

was stacked with grilled salmon bacon tomato, lettuce and two slices of wheat bread cut in half, the price was $16.00 dollars, not including a drink and it was all worth the 16 bucks! Again I'm in Martha's Vineyard, I'm loving working here but I can't afford to live here, not yet but maybe one day in the future, also did I mention that the theater was up the street further, it's called the film Center, it has 177 seats, Mr. Mullins wife told us that it opened in 2012. My last day at Martha's Vineyard caring for the Mullins was Feb 29, 2017. (We all have guilt and shame or we wouldn't be human). That's why we should, show class, have pride, and display honesty, wherever we go. Do all good you can, by all means in all ways you can, in all the places you can, to all people you can, as long as you can, a strong positive self-image is the best possible preparation. Doing your best sometimes, is more important than being the best. Define _____ yourself to be, what no other can be, do what no other can exactly do. Having a good honest lifestyle to me means, to put god first, get enough sleep, eat healthy foods, which I know is hard to do, but it can be done.! Plan to study or read the bible, or a good book, be positive, don't be a procrastinator, like I was, if you make a commitment, try to stick to your word, because at the end of the day, that's all you have, is your word of mouth for people to trust, always be prepared, it's about self-discipline, stay on track of what you are doing, it's about organization. (We must learn to live together, as brothers, or perish together as fools. Dr. Martin Luther King,) (Were all different, but still a beautiful world/ different people, different beliefs, different hopes, different dreams, our

previous President Jimmy Carter said it best! By taking responsibility we make our world better. We should make the most out of every opportunity we have. A saying now is, don't wait for your ship to come in, go out and get it! The reason why is, because so many people have wasted their whole lives, waiting on someone or something,  when they can get up off their rear ends and make their situation much much better, with god's help, and not depending on another human being. We as a people must be the change, we see in this world.! We have a right to feel safe, and a responsibility to look out for others, we've all been blessed so let's pass it on, said patti labelle, and that's one true fact! You are now blessed for reading this book about a child that had nothing, grew up without Knowing her loving mother, to teach her anything, or help guide her through life, but she still survived, and grew up in a world she never knew. We all have cares, & problems, we cannot solve alone, but if we go to our god in prayer, we are never alone, this is what I had to do for the rest of my life. A wise man listen to advice (proverbs 12;15). we as a people cannot live without wisdom and knowledge. This book will also be dedicated to my lovely grandkids. grandma loves you, more than life! Because you are part of my life!. This is Another day I've lived to see, today June 4th, 2013. *I Have a steady job now, living in alpharetta Ga, taking care of my senior client, which also has sundowners, this is something I've been doing for the past 19 years, taking care of the sick, and caring those who can't help themselves, I love my job! because If we live long enough,  we might be walking in*

*there shoes, because you never Know, what your end will be like, I've been on this job now for since, Mar 3, 2013,, well today is June 19,2013, and I just received a call from my agency that my nursing license has been renewed for another two years, June 30,2013, will be 20 years in the nursing field, I'm not tired yet, 10 more years to work, then I can retire, but for now I'm loving taking care of those who can't care for themselves, my Passion is caring for others, and making their life as comfortable as possible as long they live, being a Caregiver nurse you have to have Patience, kindness, and a lot of love for your people, because some of them have no knowledge of what they are saying, and can't remember what they are doing from day to day, so you have to be there eyes, hands, and ears, to make your day go smoothly, looking out back at the lovely Lake, it's about a mile and half long, looking at the moving water and boats, makes you think a lot, about important things in your life, the giusses and there young moving along the waves of the water, after the rain they come in the yard, to feed on the worms, just above the banks of the water, near the boat dock, looking at these babies are a site to see. When Michael Jackson died, in 2009 on that day a goose laid five eggs, Now there babies, are big and healthy, I heard people killed themselves when Michael died, according to the KJV bible, they will not be forgiven for self murder, When all they had to do was pray,! Lord when I don't see my way, I felt like giving up, You gave me grace, when I lost my friend, when I lost my Job, you gave me grace, You let me see*

*a brighter day, and showed me your grace, all I had to do, was kneel and pray, and say thank you Lord! for your Grace, you had mercy on my Soul, I can't take my life, Because you gave up your life!! So that I may live, Thank you Lord! Thank you for your grace, have mercy on Michael soul! Because we don't know, what he was thinking, when he left this life. I pray that his soul will see your guiding light! So Many other celebrities has left this life, god only knows what was going on in there lives, we should not be judgemental against anyone, But just ask god to have mercy on their souls and ours!, then we can live better lives! Be happier and have more sympathy towards others. I have a nephew that I pray for daily, he doesn't know it but I do, because of his lifestyle, he's done more than 10 years in prison, lived thru that, came out and was shot multiple times, I prayed so hard on my knees, for god to bring him out of the pain he was in, when I saw him lying in the hospital bed, looking like his mother Wanda, and his father which is my oldest brother, I cried like a baby, but I knew it was nothing the doctors or me could do, I even asked the nurse why was his head swollen, and his eye cut, and swollen shut, dried blood was still on the side of his head, she told me that he came in that way, and that they were only treating him for the bullet wounds, he's 31 now, and he has been through a lot in his 30 years, but he will always have a praying Aunty, I pray for my son and all the young men in my family, for god to always shield and protect them, because sometimes they can't protect themselves. That's why we should*

*pray going out and coming in, get rid of misery and dread, give up supposing the worst things, and look for the best instead! Today look for the good in people, and when you walk down the street, smile at the people you meet, your life will be twice as sweet! Happy is the man who finds wisdom, and the man who gets understanding, As I said before, we all have problems, and cares we cannot solve alone, but if we go to god in private we are never alone! Never be too busy to stop and recognize, the grief that lies in another's eyes, too busy to help, care or sympathize, seek to forgive and forget, imagined hurts, that have come your way. Be thankful for pleasant memories. Stop awhile and reminisce on pleasant, happy little things you used to do, today I'm thankful for pleasant memories, the nature of our attitude, toward circumstantial things, determines our acceptance of the problems that life brings. I'm closing this chapter of my life and beginning a new one! It doesn't take a new year, to make a new start! In loving memory of those I love so dearly My Mom whom I never knew, and my father, which I knew somewhat, but loved him dearly until his end, All my loving aunts, near and far, I love you dearly, with all my heart, To my aunts that are 70 and above, the oldest is 82, still going to Hospitals and praying for family members that are sick, cling to your standards, because you fought a good fight, take a firm stand, for things that are right, because you can always get a pray through to God, even if when we can't, (I love you all ! Lynn.) My aunt Bernice was the one that took a firm stand, and*

*fought for me and my siblings, told my dad the preacher to his face, because everyone else was afraid of him, he was wrong and his kids were right, that indeed they had been mistreated by some people in their lives, thank you aunty for standing for our rights, when we were just kids, trying to live life! (We love You) The Second part of this book will be coming in the near future, so keep[reading! tell the truth shame the devil! tell your story ! Because no one else can, this is the autobiography of Ms. Melinda Johnson Clark. known as (Lynn) Bishop Daughter.*

103

Lightning Source UK Ltd.
Milton Keynes UK
UKHW012104060120
356462UK00002B/667/P